So That's Who I Am

by

Chauncey Smith

TEACH Services, Inc.
P U B L I S H I N G
www.TEACHServices.com • (800) 367-1844

Copyright © 2017 Chauncey Smith

Copyright © 2017 TEACH Services, Inc.

ISBN-13: 978-1-4796-0725-9 (Paperback)

ISBN-13: 978-1-4796-0726-6 (ePub)

ISBN-13: 978-1-4796-0727-3 (Mobi)

Library of Congress Control Number: 2017902692

TEACH Services, Inc.
P U B L I S H I N G
www.TEACHServices.com • (800) 367-1844

Thank You

Gary and Nancy Holtz:
For being there before-during and now for me,
parents and family.

Andre Landzaat, *Actor*:
You won the award for best Villain on General Hospital yet you
couldn't have been a better friend to me for over 35 years.

Aunt Carol Stewart:
For picking up the phone when Bina called. You have sent me a
Birthday and Christmas cards every year since.

Writer and Friend: **Steven Mosley**

Faith For Today and **TV's Lifestyle Magazine Team**:
My work family.

Monique Roy, Greg West, David Sojka, and **Bradon Schwarz**
for your support and advice.

To GOD be the GLORY!!!

Table of Contents

Foreword

I have known Chauncey for over 20 years now. There are people that you meet along this crazy journey of life and you say "yep, we get each other." Our conversations began really when Don and I adopted our youngest child, who is now 21. Chauncey was adopted as well, and had just begun to find pieces of his story in the way of getting more information about his biological family. And this intrigued me. I wanted to know everything. Not just for our youngest son, but for my husband Don as well, who was adopted too.

As I began to see Chauncey's story unfold, I was one of his biggest cheerleaders. We all need to know where we've come from, so that we know where we can go.

I'm quite thrilled that Chauncey has written his story down for generations to come—which is important. But to see the story unfold inside of Chauncey has been a joy and privilege as one of the friends honored enough to walk along side him.

Thank you my friend, for sharing your story. We are all better because of it.

— Sandi Patty

Sandi Patty is the most awarded female vocalist in contemporary Christian music history, with Five Grammy Awards, 40 Dove Awards and over eleven million units sold.

Chapter 1

Rendezvous

Chauncey to Ohio

LA to Chicago, across vast stretches of Western desert and Midwestern wheat field, was pretty much a blank. He would hardly remember it. But after taking off from O'Hare toward Columbus, it started hitting Chauncey hard. "When I land, I'm gonna see my mom." That thought blacked out everything else—the landscape, the weather, fellow passengers. He could only think about laying eyes on the person with whom he'd been having surreal, intense, revealing phone conversations.

Chauncey took deep breaths. He could actually feel his blood pressure rising. And he kept tossing up a prayer: "Lord, just help me get through this without breaking down."

A woman flying home to see her family, seated beside him, noticed his distress. "Are you OK?"

Chauncey looked over at her, then gushed the whole story.

She started crying.

So, Chauncey asked a favor. "Would you videotape me walking off the plane—meeting her?"

By the time the plane parked at a gate in Columbus, Chauncey's seatmate had phoned her family to tell them what was about to happen. Other passengers had overheard and started wishing him well as he stood shakily to his feet.

Chauncey: "There's No Way, Really, to Describe Your Emotions"

There's no way, really, to describe your emotions. Most everyone knows what it's like to, say, get married, lose a friend, attend a reunion. Those scenes are portrayed over and over in books and movies. The related feelings are all nicely labeled. But, after more than three decades, meeting the woman who gave me birth? What's that about? It's such a jumble of excitement, fear, devotion, anxiety, regret. You don't know where you are. You're floating in space, weightless, desperately trying to find something to grab.

Chauncey willed himself down the long, long Jetway. His newfound friend hurried ahead with the video camera, calling back to him about what a nervous wreck she was. His life, so far anyway, was passing before him. When he stepped out into the terminal, people were actually applauding, cameras flashing, as if a celebrity were making an appearance. Word had gotten around fast.

It was a blur for a few seconds as Chauncey glanced around at all the faces huddled there. And then he saw one. *The* one. All the fuzziness turned to tunnel vision. For the first time in his life, Chauncey Smith looked into a face that reflected his own.

Loretta to California

Loretta enjoyed the typical warm, happy feelings for the first few months. Regret didn't show its face at all. She was pregnant.

Life was growing inside her. It didn't seem complicated. When girlfriends patted her stomach and shared their congratulations, she took it in gratefully.

Only one thing: she didn't have any names picked out.

And after six months, that one thing grew into a reality check. Loretta was very young. Unmarried. Not in love. Without money. And there was no family support on which she could rely.

Those facts kept pressing in on her. They wouldn't let up.

Yes, she'd known the father for years; they'd dated off and on. But she now realized they just weren't meant to be a couple.

In the middle of many nights, rolling over with her big stomach, thoughts shot through her, laying out emotions at random. Why hadn't her friends asked her why she hadn't bought a crib yet? What kind of life would her child have? Why hadn't she been more careful?

Loretta pondered the options. It was all about her situation, not about her child. So, she decided to choose adoption. And once she decided, young Loretta put her heart and soul into the process. She would find the best possible parents for her baby, the best possible life. She had to keep telling herself, "This will help someone; this will really help someone," because the baby would kick once in a while, because her body was nurturing this child every minute.

So, Loretta flew to California. Had the baby. And a doctor there told her about a very nice couple who was looking for a child.

One thing Loretta knew she had to avoid. She wouldn't be able to look at the baby. She wouldn't be able to touch the baby. If that happened, she'd never be able to give him away.

Marilyn and Chuck to the San Fernando Valley

Marilyn met Chuck.

They fell in love.

They hadn't been able to have a child yet but weren't too worried about it. They weren't trying *not* to have a child. But at the time, they weren't desperate for a family either.

Then Marilyn got a job in a newborn nursery at a small hospital in the San Fernando Valley near Los Angeles. From time to time obstetricians would ask her if she and Chuck would be interested in adopting a baby. They knew the Smiths didn't have any kids.

For some reason, Marilyn didn't take any of the offers. She was still haunted by her first pregnancy. Everything had gone wrong. The baby had died.

One day, a female obstetrician Marilyn greatly respected came to her with another bit of news: "I have this woman who's going to deliver a baby; all the signs are its healthy, no problems. The mother's very nice."

Marilyn told the doctor she had some neighbors who'd just lost a pregnancy. They might be interested.

"Well, sure, ask them."

So, one Friday, Marilyn told this couple, who'd become good friends, about the baby on the way.

They asked to think about it over the weekend.

Well, that Saturday and Sunday, Marilyn and Chuck talked about the coming of this child, and the possibility of starting a family began nudging them. By Monday, they were telling each other, "If they don't take this baby, maybe we should."

They didn't feel that ready. But something seemed to be knocking on their door.

When the neighbor couple declined, the knock grew louder.

Marilyn told her obstetrician colleague, "Chuck and I think we want to adopt."

The woman took one look at Marilyn, smiled, and said, "Sold."

They only had a month to prepare.

The next-door neighbors who were going to adopt Chauncey became lifelong friends with Chuck and Marilyn. Nancy and Gary would also adopt two children of their own and Chauncey, Charmaine, and Barry grew up playing with their kids. Funny to think, either way, God wanted Chuck and Marilyn in Chauncey's life.

Endings

Chauncey's journey was going to have a remarkable ending. And yet he would bounce against other endings at the same time: a best friend who balked at the journey and stared in anguish at an electric cord hanging in his closet; a sister who did want to take the journey but would remain haunted by a face that just wouldn't appear to her.

Something to Know: What You Really Hear

We're different.

Almost all people who are adopted feel different—unshakably different. Their adoptive parents can love and support them, treat them as their very own. But there's still something different.

It registers on some level. After all, the most important time of a person's life are the earliest years. Those first days. Surely, they mattered. You weren't held by the woman in whose stomach you lived. After months of living in your mom's womb, you are then separated from her. The woman who gave you life never holds, touches, or loves you.

Is all this just in your imagination? You don't quite believe it.

You've got a mother and father. And yet…

Different doesn't mean better or worse—it just means different. And you tend to think about it all the time.

"What if I grew up in another state? Another school? What if I had another set of friends? Another set of brothers and sisters? Would I have different interests, different hobbies? Would I be happier, skinnier, have more hair, have less of a belly? Would I be such a worrywart?" Yeah, you can't help thinking about all kinds of stuff.

And the biggest difference is simply this: you don't look like anybody else in your world.

It hits you at family gatherings. Everybody's always talking about how this kid takes after Aunt Jillian and that kid is the spitting image of Uncle Jack. Some new baby even reflects a bit of Grandmother's eyes. In Chauncey's case, it was usually about his brother, Barry. He was the "real son," the one not adopted, the kid Marilyn gave birth to after adopting Chauncey and Charmaine, thinking she couldn't get pregnant. Yes, there was a lot of talk about how much Barry looked like his father.

You interact. You do the barbecue. You play games with your cousins. It's all quite normal on the outside. But you can't shake this little bug in your ear telling you you're still different.

Once in a while, there might even be a little teasing about being left on a doorstep or rescued from a dumpster. But the faces are what keep picking on you. You can't help but look for something to latch onto in a chin here, a cheek there, a laugh, a gesture.

And you keep coming up empty. There's even a shadow of illegitimacy lurking somewhere nearby.

You don't have a resemblance, but what you do have is a question that haunts: Just what did that giving away do to me? What mark did it leave on me? Chauncey, for example, couldn't help imagining the unbelievable amount of emotion and stress involved the moment his mother made up her mind to give her baby away. And since he seemed to feel emotions and stress more strongly than the people around him, he came to believe that those intense, conflicted feelings were instantly inherited by him at birth. They were passed on somehow. And he would carry them, in various ways, the rest of his life.

You don't have a resemblance, but what you do have is a question that haunts: Just what did that giving away do to me?

He also tried to imagine something else. Surely, Bio Mom gave him away because she loved him so much. She made the sacrifice because, in her situation, this was the best she could do for that child.

So an adopted person often drifts in this no-man's-land, between feeling some distant stress and assuming a distant love. Which will win out? Will the adopted person fall into blaming every hurtful experience in his or her life on that giving away? Or will he or she grow into a deeper acceptance of people having to make difficult choices?

So, what can friends and family of the adopted do? Your arm around a shoulder, your affectionate phrases, your little acts that put a child *in* a family—all those things take on special weight for an adopted kid. They mean more. They have more value. And letting them slip by makes an even bigger difference. For example, saying something like, "We couldn't have any of our own so we had to adopt" or, "We had two of our own then adopted" puts the adopted child on a different level. Instead, build the adopted child up by saying, "We have three kids—I can't even remember which one is adopted."

Chapter 2
Bina

Bina Almilli talked to Chauncey about everything. They'd been friends for nineteen years, ever since they were just out of high school when he'd walked into a Taco Bell (where she was the assistant manager), looking for an easy way to get pocket money.

Bina knew all about Chauncey growing up. He had wonderful parents. She sometimes wished she had parents like Marilyn and Chuck. She was only a few years older. It was like they'd come of age together, like brother and sister. And once in a while she'd ask him if he ever thought about trying to find his birth parents. He'd think about it for a moment, then kind of wave it off. Chauncey had become friends with some makeup artists who worked on *General Hospital* and then fallen in with most of the cast. This high school kid partied regularly with soap stars who were trailed by thousands of adoring fans across America. For several years, he lived large in Hollywood.

Bina knew how much this meant to a kid who always knew he was different. It was like the boy had found another family, complete with paparazzi, gushing interviews, and stretch limousines. And she was also happy when he got a real job marketing Christian television shows at a large media center.

Chauncey seemed to have it made in his thirties. An independent, successful single guy with a very wide circle of friends. But on some quiet days, while Bina and Chauncey reminisced about their lives, the question still came up—especially when Chauncey admitted there was still something missing.

One afternoon, Bina was talking about how difficult it was to put closure on her marriage. So much stuff still dangled between her and Todd.

Chauncey perked up. "It's kind of like me. I was adopted; I'd like to put closure on that, if I could."

Bina was rather shocked at first. He'd never mentioned this much before. How come he hadn't talked about this? They talked about *everything*. Didn't seem to be an issue.

So, she asked, "Do you ever want to try to find the woman who gave you birth?" Before, Chauncey had always talked about how hard, how intimidating the task seemed. He thought the chances of it resulting in a good outcome were probably slim. But leaning back on the circular sofa in Bina's living room that day, Chauncey become more reflective. He got a look on his face Bina hadn't seen before. Slowly putting his hands to his chest, Chauncey said quietly, "Well, it would be wonderful to see a photograph of someone who looks like you."

That did it. Bina decided she would find Chauncey's other mother. She would track her down, whatever it took.

The Search Begins

Chauncey had one thing: a birth certificate for Baby Boy Marrison. The report of the physician attending the birth of a child placed for adoption. But the information about the birth mother had been blacked out. All Chauncey could make out was, "Mental health: above average. No infectious diseases during pregnancy."

Not much to go on.

Bina: "I Never Had to Pretend I Was Someone Else"

Chauncey told me up-front he could only work weekdays. Nights and weekends were reserved for his *General Hospital* clan. He wanted just enough money to pay his bills. And he didn't follow the rules too well. Sometimes I'd get mad when he put too much of the good stuff in a burrito for a "special customer." He'd slip his shoes off while taking an order at the counter, a big no-no. Or he might slip a fake mouse under my chair. Sometimes I got so frustrated I'd have to go outside and sit on my cooling-off rock.

But pretty soon we had customers who started bringing us cookies, who started calling us by name. And everybody who came by wanted to know where Chauncey was. So he was good for business. Besides, what other Taco Bell had signed photos of *General Hospital*'s Luke and Laura on the wall?

And sometimes I'd go to some soap-star event. It was pretty heady. Chauncey's circle kept widening. He'd be talking on the phone, look at me, and have someone like Shirley Jones say hi.

When Chauncey stepped into my fast-food world, I was the boss. When I stepped into his Hollywood world, *he* was the boss. I can't remember all the celebrities I met. But the special thing was that I could always be just me around them. I never had to pretend I was someone else.

But there were two signatures on the adoption papers. One read "Loretta Mae Marrison," while the other read "Loretta Mae Martin." She was twenty-one and from somewhere back East. She came from Ohio.

Bina figured Marrison was a more likely name to pursue. A woman born in 1942.

Then Bina ran across the second page of the hospital record—and managed to copy it. The sheet noted Loretta Mae Martin's blood type and birth date. She had a brother and sister. She was healthy, Caucasian, Methodist. A high school graduate. Her father was a mechanic from North Carolina. She had red hair. She played the accordion.

That last little bit of info stood out. Maybe that was the key. How many Marrisons played the accordion, after all? Well, there were probably a lot of them. But Bina kept this list in front of her at all times and began making calls.

She started calling Marrisons in Ohio and North Carolina. Every day. Sometimes it was one call. Sometimes it was fifty. Sometimes she'd look on the Internet. There were thousands of Marrisons, of course, with thousands of addresses and phone numbers. She tried looking for a Loretta Mae, or an L. Marrison, or an L. and R. Marrison. Nothing.

But one lady Bina spoke to, Debbie Marrison, was also working on a family tree. And she proved to be quite helpful. She gave Bina useful ideas about finding people and suggested that focusing on middle names was actually an easier route sometimes. Debbie told Bina not to give up. And Bina felt something spiritual from this stranger's words of encouragement.

One day, Bina decided just to call Marrisons at random rather than go down her long, long list in order. And the first person who answered the phone gave her some names, people who might be related—there was a Fred and Ethel Marrison, and a Luci. Luci and Ethel were sisters. That struck Bina. Chauncey was the biggest *I Love Lucy* fan in the world; he knew all about Lucy's neighbors, Fred and Ethel. Wouldn't it be funny if these people were the key to finding Loretta? It seemed to Bina to be a sign.

Making other calls, Bina discovered that Luci and Fred had passed away. But Ethel led her to a woman named Carol Stewart, formerly Carol Marrison.

Bina called Carol, saying she was helping a friend with family history, putting some closure in his life. Bina asked Carol, "Do you have a sister?"

"Yes."

"Is her name Loretta Mae?"

Now it was all Bina could do to keep from screaming. She didn't want to scare the woman away. But she did get Loretta's address in Stanfield, North Carolina.

Still, Bina needed to be sure. So, she called Carol a few days later. She mentioned that her friend Chauncey had been adopted.

She was looking at the Marrison family tree and had some additional questions.

"What about religion? Catholic? Protestant?"

"All are Protestant," Carol replied

"What about physical characteristics? Do red hair and fair complexions run in your family?"

"Yes, all three of us had red hair—when we were younger," she chuckled.

"So you are the oldest, then Loretta, then William?"

"Yes, I'll be sixty-one next month, but their ages…"

"You said Loretta was born in 1942?"

"That's correct."

"What about special interests? Start with Loretta."

"I know she took piano lessons many years ago, and she plays the accordion by ear, used to enjoy singing a little…"

"Really?" Now Bina's hands were sweating on the phone. This is her! It just has to be! She fought to sound calm. "Now Carol, your mother was a housewife and your father a construction worker, right?"

"Correct."

Now Bina felt very confident. "Carol, I must tell you something. After our conversation last week, I was able to track down Loretta Mae and was able to get her phone number."

"How did you get her phone number?"

"I got it from the Internet. Carol, I need to be up-front with you. During all my research, I really wanted my path to end at Loretta, for reasons I'll tell you now. Please be patient."

Carol now sounded a little hesitant. "OK."

"OK, here goes. Before I begin the story, can you please tell me if Loretta Mae was in California for a short period back in 1963?"

"Yes." Carol sounded even quieter. "She was with our aunt."

"Was that aunt Ethel March?"

"I think that's who she stayed with."

"OK. Did Loretta give birth to a baby boy on October 1, 1963, during her stay in California?"

A big sigh rolled through the phone. "Yes, she did."

"Carol, the friend I'm doing research for is that baby boy, now thirty-five years old. His name is Chauncey Smith."

"Oh, my."

Something to Know: The Way You Persist

All the time Bina was playing Sherlock Holmes, Chauncey still didn't think he could get any kind of closure; he couldn't even imagine it. But Bina kept looking. And the fact is, at that time,

Bina: "I Had to Act"

I followed my heart with every single phone call, whether it opened a door or led to a brick wall. It was a matter of just following your gut feeling. One of the surprising things was how many people I ran across who listened to my story and wanted to help. There were a lot more of them than people who didn't want to talk about it.

You do get rejection. You will run into quite a few dead ends before you find the right road. Sometimes it's one step forward, when you think you have a lead, and then two steps back. But I just kept moving on to the next possibility. You can't tell a person who's still struggling with his adoption, after many years, "Just get over it." Even the best kind of words wasn't going to do anything. There was only one way I could really help. I had to act. And I believed that, eventually, something would pop up.

There was only one way I could really help. I had to act.

everything was up in the air in her life. She'd gone through a divorce. So, she focused on this one task. Her life, as she knew it, was ending. But maybe another life was beginning.

This woman was keenly aware of how much someone else's life was bouncing around in her hands. So she asked Chauncey over and over, "Are you OK? Will you be OK with the outcome, whatever it is? Shall I keep pursuing this?"

She always got the green light.

Through the whole roller coaster ride of this search—picking up promising signs and running into brick walls—Bina persisted. And through her persistence, she kept finding helpful people.

Bina's experience in the search suggests that a person's attitude is more important than the mechanics of the search. In looking for a biological parent, it's what's in your heart that leads to success even more than any sophisticated technique.

Bina made sure she was both persistent and respectful. She believed Chauncey had a right to seek out Bio Mom. But other people also had a right to their private lives.

Bina never called people without giving information about herself—who she was, what she was doing, why she was doing it. And she kept that information consistent, from one person to the next. She always told them she'd be happy to answer any questions they had.

In looking for a biological parent, it's what's in your heart that leads to success even more than any sophisticated technique.

A person looking for a biological parent is going to be desperate for information. The tendency is to grab hold of any promising name or place with a vengeance. And it's easy to sound demanding.

Bina made sure she didn't just blurt things out. She knew she had to build some trust with the people who might have leads to Bio Mom.

She also took notes diligently about everything people said. These helped her focus more clearly through the roller coaster ride. She recognized that one little clue over here might match up with another little clue over there and take her somewhere.

And yes, Bina's search did take her somewhere, somewhere that would impact a lot of people's lives.

This is the FIRST picture together, taken at the airport.

Chapter 3
Loretta

The phone rang early one morning and Loretta picked it up to hear a stranger's voice.

"Hello, may I please speak to Mrs. Loretta Mae Marrison Martin?"

Her long name sounded a little odd to her. "Speaking."

"Hope I'm not calling at a bad time."

"Not at all."

"Well, I've been doing some research on a family tree. So far, everyone I've spoken to has been so friendly and patient. Last week I spoke to your sister Carol Stewart. Did she mention I called?"

Now Loretta remembered. It was someone from California. A vague fear started welling up in her stomach. "Yes, she told me. Although she said she gave you my address, not my phone number."

"Right. She felt a little uncomfortable giving that information out. I found your number on the Internet, hope you don't mind."

"No, I don't mind, you just never know these days…"

"I've actually been doing research on behalf of a good friend of mine."

Loretta thought she'd better do some checking herself. "Could I first get some information from you? Could I have your name?"

Bina gave it and said she'd be happy to answer any questions.

"And the friend you're doing this for? His name?"

"Chauncey Smith." She also gave his address and phone number.

"Oh, my. California. Calling from so far away." Now the fear started welling up in Loretta's throat. She asked, "Is your friend part of the Marrison clan?"

"Well, this is where my search becomes a bit more complicated."

"Oh. dear. OK."

"I'll start from the beginning if you don't mind. My friend was adopted. Born October 1, 1963. Within the past few years, he's wanted to put some type of closure to this part of his life."

Now the fear was choking Loretta. She'd stopped breathing. A hundred thoughts and emotions bounced around in her head. What was happening? This was her baby boy! She hadn't ever told her daughters about that birth. What must he think of her now?

This was her baby boy!

Bina tried her best to cover the silence. "He's wanted to do this research so he can let his biological mother know that he is OK, has a very successful life, a wonderful family. And most importantly, he wants to say thank you. Maybe even get a photograph as a keepsake."

More silence. Loretta still couldn't fight through it all. The giving up she'd made decades ago, all coming back suddenly in one phone call. The nights of wondering about him. The birthdays she'd thought about. Her son. Her only son. He'd grown up a complete mystery, of course, but one she could never really let go.

Bina tried again. "Chauncey and I have been going back and forth about the best way to approach this. And we decided, since I've been speaking to everyone, I would make the first call."

The only thing Bina could here was a faint sigh.

She kept going. She quickly relayed how their search began. The adoption paper signatures. The birth in California. "I have to be honest. I wanted my path to lead to you. I was hoping that I have found the Loretta Mae Marrison Martin that I've been searching for."

Loretta didn't think she could choke up even more. But she did. For two whole minutes. The longest two minutes of her life. Fighting to say yes to the boy she hadn't seen for thirty-five years. But she was held back by the shock, the unknown, the world of complication this might bring her family.

Bina waited, desperately patient. And finally asked, "Are you OK?"

Loretta murmured a barely audible assent.

"Can you please tell me if you gave birth to a baby boy?"

Agony. Confusion. But the word came out, "No."

"You were never in California?"

Another gut-wrenching struggle against the word she spoke: "No."

Bina thanked Loretta for her time and asked her to call if she had any helpful information.

When Loretta hung up the phone, it felt like an anvil dropping on her head. She collapsed in her chair.

Loretta had to walk through her anguish for several days. A part of her knew she simply had to reach out to this boy, now a man, to whom she'd given birth. A part of her was determined to shield the rest of her family, especially her daughters, from any news that might disturb them, might upset their picture of growing up with Mom. And what about her husband, Richard, the father of her four daughters? How was he supposed to take this news? There was a human being walking around who had emerged from a relationship long ago she shouldn't have been in.

She couldn't talk about it with anyone. She pondered it in the middle of every night. She was nervous all day. For her, the big burden was that she'd denied this part of her motherhood to her daughters. That's the way she looked at it.

There were flashbacks to the first time she held her first grand-child, Rita's baby boy. It was like holding the son she'd given up. Yes, she always knew in her heart of hearts it was a boy, even though she'd never seen the child. He was taken away right at delivery. And she hadn't thought of a name for him. After marrying Richard, she'd told him, "If we have a boy, let's call him Ross Reed." That was the boy name that had come to her too late.

Loretta had heard plenty of self-help talk in her life. She wasn't unaware of that important bit of conventional wisdom: it's always good to talk about it. But what she knew instinctively was that talking about it multiplies the feelings, it brings the distant past right into the pit of your present stomach.

Finally, however, she just couldn't stand another hour going by before the truth was known. First, Loretta just laid it out before Richard. He was amazingly casual about it. For him, it was a story from decades ago. Interesting but not threatening. And yeah, why not make contact with the kid?

Loretta hoped and prayed there wasn't something else going on behind her husband's easy smile.

Then Loretta called her eldest daughter, Rita, and asked her to come over.

Loretta and Richard seemed unusually quiet out on the back deck. Loretta obviously had something on her mind, and she kept walking back into the kitchen to fidget with something. Finally, Richard said, "Mom has something she needs to tell you."

Loretta tried to bring up the subject, obviously very nervous. At length, Richard put it out. "You have a half-brother."

"Oh, really?" Rita answered.

Loretta glanced over at Rita. Her daughter looked more curi-ous than shocked. That was a relief. So, she told Rita about getting pregnant at the wrong time, with the wrong man. "I was so afraid you'd be upset, mad at me, because I kept this from you and your sisters all these years."

Rita thought about it a moment. "How could I be mad to find out I have a brother? That's kind of cool."

Loretta needed to sit down. A huge weight had been taken off her shoulders. She filled in more of the story, about staying with

Rita's aunt and uncle in the LA area. Giving birth. Never really seeing the baby. Finding out good things about this couple that wanted to adopt.

And this brother of hers, Chauncey, had been on a quest to find his biological mother. Loretta reviewed the phone call from Bina.

"He lives in California," Loretta said. There was still a lot of uncertainty in her voice.

Rita replied quickly, "Great, you need to contact him; we need to have him in our life."

Fortunately, the other three daughters reacted in basically the same way. They were grown up. Their lives were pretty much shaped. And now they had this accessory, an actual blood brother. Interesting. Cool.

The emotion all of them expressed was sadness that their poor mother had had to live with this, by herself, all these years.

Loretta didn't gush out the truckload of feelings that came by every time she brought up this subject. She didn't want to dump all that on her daughters. So much lay in her heart she couldn't even begin to describe. But she did grab hold of this: her daughters were OK. Thank God her daughters were OK.

The Destination

It was seven on a Saturday morning when a phone call woke Bina in her home. Could it be her husband, Todd? Bina picked up the phone. A groggy Bina heard the words, "A lady by the name of Loretta."

Bina jumped up. Sleep vanished. Surely, this was Bio Mom!

"Hi, Loretta."

Bina felt the nervous excitement well up in her voice. But Loretta's voice had such a soothing quality it sounded like a completely different person from the woman she'd conversed with before. That's because Loretta had settled something in her heart. She was going back thirty-five years. Yes, she was finally going to touch that baby.

There was a short pause. Then Loretta said, "I'm not a liar; I've never been a liar. I am the woman you are looking for."

There it was. The hidden treasure in the sand. Bina was tapping right on the lid of the treasure chest. Her instincts had been right. This was it, the destination. All the times she'd asked Chauncey, "Are you sure you want me to go forward, take the next step, even if there might be a disappointment?" rattled around in her head. But now they were rattling down to the bottom.

Bina was afraid she'd start crying.

Loretta continued, "I just never thought this day would ever happen. I always thought the baby's adoptive parents would never tell him he was adopted. I thought it would always be a secret for them. So, when you called, it was overwhelming; I hadn't even told my daughters."

Now Bina's excitement just gushed out. "Can Chauncey call you? Loretta, please, if it's OK, I need to call Chauncey right now. And if I can have a few moments with him, I know he'll want to call you. Or you can call him, whatever would be best for you. If I can't get hold of him, I'll call you back and let you know. Are you OK with that?"

Her soothing voice hadn't changed. "Yes, that will be fine. He may call me."

Bina thanked Loretta over and over. "Please don't go any-where."

Loretta could finally say out loud something that had been restless in her heart for decades: "I always wanted to find out what happened to my little baby boy."

A few minutes later, Bina got Chauncey on the phone. "Guess who called? Loretta! She called me! It's her. We found her."

Now all kinds of emotions rattled around inside Chauncey. He'd always thought he was prepared to hear this good news. After all, the whole journey had been toward this precise rendez-vous. But listening to Bina, Chauncey knew he wasn't really ready. How could anyone be prepared for this? And there were wild mis-givings. "Did I do the right thing? What have I started? Would there be another emotional roller coaster, more painful suspense if this woman got cold feet?"

Bina was telling him, "Call her. Call her. Your mom is waiting for your call."

But what Chauncey thought of first was the mother who had raised him. Marilyn. He had to talk to her.

Something to Know: Happy Endings Aren't Effortless

When you read this book, you get the story flowing from one chapter to the next. What you don't know is that this chapter took many months to get down. Sharing the story was one of the hardest things Loretta Marrison ever had to do. It took her several months to get up the courage to share. So many fears seemed to paralyze her.

It had been easy for Marilyn to talk about the whole process. It felt natural.

It was far more complicated for Loretta.

Chauncey could feel the nervousness in her voice when they talked about setting up an interview with Steven, a writer and friend who helped with this book, about the details. She wanted to arrange a time when she could talk freely with Steven when none of her family were present. She wanted time to prepare.

Chauncey explained that her chapter was all about the love she had for him, and that it would help people who were adopted and their families. There are so many mothers out there who've gone through just what she's gone through. And her story just might be the key that helps people fill that void in their lives and the lives of their children. It might even help some put their lives back together again.

Loretta acknowledged all this and thanked Chauncey for his encouragement. But it held for her a fear that even he couldn't fully understand. The details of the past have a way of spilling out in the present. And sometimes pain is in the details. How would it all impact her husband, her daughter, her whole family? How would it affect people she hadn't even met?

She couldn't help thinking of people judging her, comparing her story other stories. The part of her life that was the hardest to talk about was about to be exposed. Things that had burrowed so deep would now surface in print.

The thing that made it hardest for Loretta was simply guilt. It was inescapable. No matter how many times someone goes over the circumstances, no matter how many good things people try to say about the adoption, it's there.

And what terrified Loretta the most was the idea that something she might say could hurt Chauncey. Her explaining the specifics of that time when she gave him up—how could that not cause him pain? And that seemed unbearable. Hadn't she done enough already?

Chauncey also found something unbearable: adding to Bio Mom's guilt. He didn't want to say anything that might cut into long-buried feelings. He didn't want to do anything that would make the parents who raised him feel guilty, either.

And yet, weren't they all on a journey? Wasn't honesty the way for everyone to reach that closure, that sense of resolution?

Chauncey had to come to terms with that ugly word: *abandonment*. It was there, whether he talked about it or not. It was there, whether it had a rational explanation or not. And sometimes it seemed the first fact of his life, maybe even an experience. Maybe that's why he could be so controlling at times. Maybe that's why he grasped at certain friendships so tightly.

So finally, Chauncey and Steven sent ten questions to Loretta. Chauncey had ten thousand. He never ran out. He didn't want to put pressure on Loretta. He had to remind himself that he wasn't the number one priority in this Marrison family just because he showed up. He didn't have rights greater than other people's. And yet so much of him wanted to understand Loretta's thoughts and feelings.

At one point, Chauncey tried to throw in a little humor. "I know this is hard for you, but just think of it as, 'Hey, I missed all those years of Chauncey stressing me out as a teenager, and now I can finally get something really tough from him.' You think these questions are hard, imagine all the trouble I could have brought you before."

Chauncey was afraid the joke wouldn't go over well, but, at length, Bio Mom managed to come up with answers. It happened on one of Chauncey's visits. He'd waited the whole weekend to bring out the questions. But finally, out on the back porch, sipping ice tea in the heat and humidity of North Carolina, he plunged ahead.

Chauncey just had to ask, very nervously, "If you had to do it all over again, what would you do?"

Loretta was silent for a while, then summoned up an honest answer. She wouldn't change anything.

Loretta knew that she'd grown up around a lot of abuse related to alcohol. And the guy she'd been with, the father of this child, showed plenty of signs of that addiction. And she just couldn't subject herself or the baby to that kind of life.

Pondering over these words later, Chauncey would realize that was the answer he hoped he would hear. It was the true love answer. It was about wishing the best for this baby, despite the most conflicted feelings imaginable.

The happy ending Chauncey found with Loretta proved to be rewarding in a way few people outside the circle of adoption can fully understand. It was deep. It was even fun.

But it didn't happen easily. Chauncey felt the effort involved during his first visit with Bio Mom. He'd brought photo albums with him. She had family photo albums to share too, and the two of them began looking through pictures on the back porch of her home in North Carolina

Chauncey stepped inside to get some coffee. When he came back through the screen door, Loretta was bawling uncontrollably.

There had been plenty of tears during their phone conversations. But these seemed different. Chauncey's first thought was, "Oh no, she's regretting our rendezvous; she's wishing I'd just go home. She's hoping she never has to see me again." It was one of those jags of irrational terror that shoot through the brain.

But Chauncey calmed himself, walked over to her, and asked, "What's the matter?"

She couldn't say. The tears were getting in the way.

But at length, she managed to explain that each page of his album was showing her what she'd missed, what she gave up. She would never know what it was like mothering that boy, at that age, that birthday, that graduation.

Now both were crying.

Richard and the daughters came out to see what the noise was about. Soon they were tearing up too. And Chauncey had a moment of recognition. "Yeah, this is where I get all my emotional stuff from. I'm not some weird guy who cries easily. It all comes from right here."

Again, Loretta had to talk about the years without contact. She thought his parents might not even tell him he was adopted. And she would never spoil that. She certainly assumed they wouldn't want him to know about her. The phone call would never come.

But now she was so thankful that it had, so thankful she could be sitting here with this thirty-five-year-old man, paging through his whole life.

Yes, there were very strong emotions. Yes, there was a big sense of loss. But in the end, it was so worth it, so worth everything.

And that's how happy endings happen. They're not like falling off a chair. They come at a price. They involve risks. There's some pain attached. But the rewards overwhelm everything else in the end.

The tears Chauncey and Loretta shared would connect them deeply as bio mom and son.

Chapter 4
Marilyn

Chauncey met with Mom and Dad, Marilyn and Chuck, at Mimi's a local restaurant in Thousand Oaks. They knew he had some kind of big news.

The first thing Chauncey did was hand them Bina's notes on her first conversation with Loretta. Poring over it, they came to the words, "No, I was never in California."

Both started tearing up. They felt the slam; their boy's hopes shattered again. But they kept reading.

Then Chauncey put a hand on the sheet of paper. "Bina got a call early this morning—from Loretta."

Marilyn saw the look on her son's face. Now the tears were flowing steadily.

The story came out. Marilyn and Chuck sat there beaming. They could feel the shovel knocking against that hidden treasure too.

Marilyn and Chuck just had to call Bina on her cell right then. Bina picked up immediately. Her phone wouldn't leave her hand that whole day. Chauncey's parents thanked her for all the work she'd done, all she'd invested in this search. Then Bina said on speaker phone, "I bet she's waiting for that call, Marilyn."

Chauncey wondered, "Should she call me?"

Marilyn knew the answer immediately, "Oh, Chauncey, *you've* got to call *her.*"

Raising Chauncey

Marilyn would always remember that first "go" contact with Loretta as a wonderful event, a historic event. Something like Apollo landing on the moon. It happened. No reservations. Chauncey's search would have a happy ending.

And it was the end of several months of anxiety.

Marilyn wasn't worried about losing her adopted son in any way. She wasn't concerned about their love changing in any way. But she was worried about Chauncey being disappointed. What if his birth mother just didn't want any contact? What if she turned out to be a rather disturbed human being?

But Chauncey was an adult. Marilyn thought him mature enough to handle it. But it would have been very different if Chauncey was, say, fourteen.

Marilyn also knew that she and Chuck always believed information about the biological mother would remain sealed. There was no official agreement. Loretta hadn't made any demands about secrecy. But in those days, secrecy was implied. You just don't track down the mother who gave the baby up for adoption. This worried Marilyn and Chuck a bit, but not nearly enough to slow down Chauncey's search.

Marilyn distinctly remembered the first printout she saw from Bina. There it was: "Loretta Mae Marrison," complete with an address and phone number. All those hours of searching had uncovered actual data.

Marilyn tried to reassure her son, who was still filled with a welter of conflicting emotions. He wondered if the news would cause problems with his birth mother's present marriage. "Oh, Chauncey, this won't be a difficult thing; I think her husband now already knows about you. It was only six weeks after Loretta gave you up for adoption at the hospital that her name changed. That's when we got the final papers, and we saw the new name, Martin, along with Marrison. And she still has that name, Martin. So, he must have known—from way back."

It had been very hard to hear about Loretta first denying that she'd ever been in California. She read it, word for word, when Chauncey handed her Bina's record of the conversation, as they were having lunch in a restaurant. The search had been building to a great climax until that point. Every contact Bina had made with a relative seemed to be taking her a step closer. And then this dramatic change felt heart-wrenching. All Bina's fears about what a disappointment regarding his bio mom might do to Chauncey came rushing back.

And yet, as the mother of three children, Marilyn didn't find it hard to put herself in Loretta's place. What a shock it must have been. Out of the blue, a stranger on the phone is talking to Loretta about her firstborn son. It was hard for Marilyn to read the words Bina had written down. She could only imagine how hard it must have been for Loretta to say them.

But a week later, the good news, the glorious news, came. Loretta had called again. She was Chauncey's bio mom. She was ready, perhaps even eager, to talk.

Chuck and Marilyn had another lunch with Chauncey. He was excited now, but more nervous than ever. What was it going to be like, talking directly to this woman?

The great news was he quickly got four different messages, from four different half-sisters, all welcoming him to the family. Marilyn thought, "How could it come out better than that?"

Since she first laid eyes on this darling baby boy at Holy Cross Hospital in Mission Hills, California, Marilyn knew nothing was ever going to change in the way she felt about him. She was a nurse who worked in delivery. She handled newborns all the time. But this baby had to be the cutest one of all.

Marilyn: "I Know My Place in Chauncey's Life"

Really, I loved the whole process right along with him. It was exciting. It was the right thing to do. To this day, I love hearing about all the things Chauncey's learning about his blood relatives, the little things he sees in his bio mom that reflect something about him. It's exciting for me too. This is my son, discovering wonderful things, becoming more whole.

He's still very anxious about every visit back to North Carolina, where they live. It actually sounds a little odd to me, how he expresses it. So many thoughts and feelings build up before the flight east. And he's always a little worried that it will bother me or disturb me in some way.

He shouldn't be, really. I know my place in Chauncey's life, and nothing's going to change that. I'm not threatened. The only way this could have been hard for me would be if Loretta just didn't want to have anything to do with him. That would have been tough to take.

That Friday was going to be her last shift; she'd resigned her position to take care of Chauncey. That Friday evening, she and husband, Chuck, picked him up.

Then there was the church they attended, the Burbank Seventh-day Adventist Church. Marilyn had already agreed weeks before to lead out in the cradle roll class.

Chuck quickly assured her, "You go; I'll be fine at home with him."

When Marilyn rushed back after church, she heard this tiny baby crying his heart out. And there was Chuck, lying beside the cradle, sound asleep.

So yes, there were adjustments to make as a new family. But it seemed they made them pretty quickly.

They would take what seemed album after album of pictures within hours. The church gave them a big shower, including new furniture. By Monday and Tuesday, Marilyn and Chuck were taking baby Chauncey all over, even grocery shopping.

They had to find another apartment, one where children were allowed. Marilyn would remember that time—it was when John Kennedy was assassinated. But though that was a jarring event for the whole country, her new baby boy loomed larger on the horizon.

As Chauncey grew up, he found one thing he excelled at: basketball. He began to show his stuff playing with other kids at Borchard Park near his home. At the age of ten, he even got acquainted with a Lakers player. Maybe he could make the big time someday. So, he wanted to join the city youth leagues.

But there was one problem. Games happened on Saturdays, and that's when the Smith family went to church. They were Seventh-day Adventists, and Saturday was their Sabbath. It was a day to be kept holy—no worldly pursuits, no secular entertainment.

So, Chauncey could play with the best of the neighborhood kids during the week, but when it really counted, in a real league on Saturday, he couldn't join them. This made him feel the odd boy out in yet another way.

He couldn't even watch the games. Chuck and Marilyn did their best to try to make this Sabbath day a pleasant family time. But Chauncey didn't want family day; he wanted to be with his friends.

Chuck did his best to make up for Saturdays. He was always quite busy as a building contractor, but he bought season tickets to Lakers games and took Chauncey down to the Forum on Tuesday and Sunday nights. He made the time. And he always let Chauncey pick out a restaurant to eat at before the game, usually Arby's or Little King Subs.

And it worked pretty well. Chauncey loved it, doing the sports thing with Dad. It wasn't so bad. Pretty normal, in fact.

But there were also some fits along the way. One Tuesday night, the Lakers were scheduled to play the Washington Bullets. Elvin Hayes and Wes Unseld were two of Chauncey's favorite players. As it turned out, Chuck had to work late at an apartment complex; they couldn't go.

Hearing about this after he got back from school, Chauncey went ballistic. He kept telling his mom, "Dad promised! Dad promised! This is the one I wanted to go to!"

Chauncey raised such a stink, in fact, that he made himself throw up.

Well, Chuck managed to make it back home in time for the two of them to rush down to LA and see the second half.

Looking back on this scene years later, Chauncey would wonder why his parents didn't just tell that bratty kid to buzz off. They never did.

And then there was Barry, Chauncey's younger brother, the surprise kid that Marilyn birthed. He was the flesh-and-blood child, of course. And an adopted child always has a keen eye for any parental favoritism.

At one point, Barry got to play ice hockey in a league with his friends. That schedule just didn't happen to conflict with Sabbath. One night, Barry even got to play at the Forum during an LA King's intermission.

Chauncey didn't let this slip by, of course. "Oh yeah," he thought, "this is the 'real' kid having a normal life in the real world." Any time Chuck and Marilyn had to say no to something Chauncey wanted to do, he could always play the guilt card: "You love Barry more." Sometimes he'd carry this thought around for days, trying to convince himself that Mom and Dad really *did* love Barry more. It was hard to buy such a line. But when Chauncey felt frustrated or angry, he gave it a shot.

Again, it's part of the regret an adopted kid will feel later. As an adult, Chauncey can imagine how painful that was for his parents to hear. It must have killed them. He hates the fact that he ever said that.

For Marilyn, her three children's different personalities popped out much more strongly than the fact that two were adopted. She could see that displayed every Halloween. Chauncey, Char, and Barry all got dressed up, all went to the same houses, all got the same candy. Char's stash would be gone in three days. Barry's would last about a month. Chauncey would keep his candy until Christmas, until some of it was so moldy he couldn't eat it.

And those distinctions—from the one who saved everything, to the one used it up right away, to the one sort of in-between— were preserved all the way to adulthood. They had their own temperaments, their own tendencies, regardless of Mom and Dad's guiding hands.

Still, Marilyn and Chuck tried their best to make sure all three kids felt cherished, felt like they belonged. If anything, they overcompensated with Chauncey and Char. Barry probably didn't get a few things he should have just because they didn't want to look like they were playing favorites.

But in the course of an adopted teenager jostling with his parents, that throwback is just too handy of a weapon. And if the kid is headstrong and wants to do what he wants to do, well, sometimes you have to duck.

Something to Know: Forgetting and Remembering

Perhaps the biggest compliment one can give Marilyn is this: Chauncey actually forgot he was adopted for weeks, sometimes months. It happened, of course, because Chuck and Marilyn treated him like a son, period. No conditions, no external strings attached. He was their boy.

It also happened when relatives managed to stumble beyond the usual lines, the usual instincts that strike adopted people so oddly and sometimes painfully. Yes, folks would talk about Marilyn and Chuck as Chauncey's mom, Chauncey's dad. Yes, sometimes they'd even throw out a comment about how much Chauncey and Barry acted alike, about ways in which Chauncey took after Chuck.

And yes, there's sometimes a fine line between blocking out and forgetting. The fact of being given up by a birth parent is always hanging there, like some scary Halloween costume in the closet. You don't look at it much. You put it on rarely. But that mysterious figure is ready to haunt at any time.

So, forgetting can be a good thing, even a warm, fuzzy thing. But remembering is never out of the picture. What a good family does is simply help an adopted child live as comfortable as possible in that place in-between. A child can be given the kind of love that makes forgetting easy. A child can also be given the kind of understanding that puts remembering in perspective.

> *A child can be given the kind of love that makes forgetting easy. A child can also be given the kind of understanding that puts remembering in perspective.*

And that can only happen if the adoptive parent has a reasonable level of security. If that parent feels threatened at all by an adoptive child's search for his or her bio mom, then forgetting is going to become impossible and remembering more complicated. Insecure parents have all kinds of ways of making a kid feel guilty for their restlessness, their wondering. Parents who see a bio mom as competition are going to make an adopted child's journey to that other home very rocky.

Marilyn displayed a wonderful kind of security as an adoptive parent. That's of incalculable value. Chauncey sensed nothing but encouragement from her in his search. She was capable of being overjoyed by a happy ending that wasn't about her. She welcomed this new extension of her son's family into her life.

It's important that the family and friends of adopted kids keep this in mind. That kid is going to be bouncing around between forgetting and remembering in his or her journey. And it's your security, your uncomplicated good wishes, that can go a long way toward making that journey a rewarding one.

Marilyn could have sent Chauncey a long, long way with just one thing she did. Soon after Chauncey talked to Bio Mom for the first time, she dug through old albums, boxed up in the closet, and helped him select pictures to send to Loretta, pictures that documented his whole life.

She even sent one of those she cherished most: an 8 × 10 of Chauncey's high school graduation.

And later, when Mother's Day came around, the first one involving two mothers, Marilyn sent Loretta a card, thanking her for that priceless gift of a baby boy. It was a way of acknowledging this woman's motherhood—and a card Loretta would always cherish.

Me and both Moms on the couch.

Chapter 5

PK

Strangely enough, *I Love Lucy* played a role in Chauncey find-ing his bio mom. It started with his bonding with *General Hospital* stars.

When he was a junior in high school, Chauncey's girlfriend, Denise, was a big *General Hospital* fan. She could never leave the house until 3:00 p.m. (after that day's episode of *General Hospital* was over). Chauncey would go over just before 3:00, hang around while she watched the end of the show, and then they'd take off. Gradually, he began coming over earlier and earlier, until he found himself, quite unexpectedly, hooked on the soap.

Months later, Chauncey and Denise heard about a *General Hospital* celebrity softball game being held for charity at Cal State LA. The stars would be playing against radio personalities. Chauncey drove down with a group of friends and watched the game, just on the other side of a chain link fence, with thousands of other screaming fans.

Before it was over, Chauncey told his friends, "I will never again be on this side of the fence." They had no idea what he was talking about.

Sometime later, another celebrity softball game came around. Chauncey went out and bought a baseball shirt with the same green and white coloring the *General Hospital* people had worn. And he put on some lettering to match the *General Hospital* logo.

Down in LA, thousands of fans were pressed against the chain link fence again. Chauncey pushed his way through in front of a security guard, who had his back to the stars warming up on the field. Chauncey pretended to be yelling a greeting to one of them and gestured to the guard. The man glanced at his baseball shirt and let him through.

Wandering over to the *General Hospital* bench, Chauncey walked up to a striking blonde he'd noticed at the previous game and introduced himself, saying he was a friend of people on the show. She turned out to be Pamela K. Cole, the soap's makeup artist. Everyone called her PK.

The two hit it off right away. She had a personality that just bounced around the dugout, and Chauncey's outgoing nature synched up with hers. Soon they were joking about all kinds of things—including the fact that Chauncey's uniform looked pretty fake.

After the last glamorous batter struck out, PK asked him, "You gonna come to the next game?"

"Yeah," Chauncey answered hopefully.

She promised to get him a pass—and a real team uniform.

PK proved to be the most powerful, opinionated, successful woman Chauncey had ever known. She was a beautiful single mom who always got what she wanted. She had had a makeup advice column for years, sometimes even making the cover of the celebrity magazines herself. And this woman, about ten years older than Chauncey, was taking him under her wing. She began inviting him to a variety of *General Hospital* events. He started playing on the softball team with the stars; they always needed nine players and sometimes one of the big names didn't show up.

Chauncey started spending more and more time on the set of the show, just hanging out with PK, getting to know the principal players. High school began to seem like a minor annoyance in his life. Chauncey always had a knack for fitting in. These stars began sending him on errands. Eventually, he became a personal assistant to some. A few times he worked as an extra on location shoots.

Chauncey got a behind-the-scenes look at plenty of big awards shows as well. Lots of stars wanted PK to do their makeup at these events.

And then there were Hollywood parties. PK didn't like to go alone; she snuck Chauncey into plenty of clubs that didn't allow anyone in under twenty-one. He found himself in a world he had only fantasized about before. PK appreciated being a part of it, too, and Chauncey could share his excitement with her. And yes, sometimes things got pretty wild. He smoked because they smoked. He drank because they drank.

Still, PK had boundaries, and she always took care of Chauncey. Her boundaries were some distance removed from the ones set up by Chauncey's Christian parents, but they were there. PK made sure Chauncey never got anywhere near drugs and didn't endanger himself while drinking, didn't get out of control. In all the craziness, she kept an eye on this eager, bright-eyed kid, soaking up the celebrity lifestyle. "I'll take care of it," was her mantra.

And PK, though an agnostic, expressed respect for Chauncey's Christian background. No one at *General Hospital* judged him for his very conservative upbringing. PK even told Chauncey she was proud of him for sticking to his beliefs—though they were rather blurry at the time.

Behind the Scenes

Chauncey had finally found his thing. It was no one else's. No one else among all the relatives gathering at family reunions and talking about who looked like who and who giggled like who and who was grumpy like who could enter this circle.

Some of Chauncey's friends were to perform at an Easter sunrise televised event at the Hollywood Bowl. He drove with a singer, Christalee, who had done some Disney film tracks and was scheduled to sing "God Bless America."

Chauncey had always wanted to see what it was like behind the scenes at the Bowl. Their VIP passes took them through the parking lot, past the talent entrance, and down a long cement hallway to the dressing rooms underground. It was very busy, very businesslike. Speakers in each dressing room cued the talent on what was happening on stage. A lot of makeup and hair. People like Rosemary Clooney vocalizing, warming up.

The headliners for this musical event were the stars of *General Hospital*, *Happy Days*, *Love Boat*, *Mork & Mindy*, *Dallas*, *Dynasty*, *Three's Company*, *The Jeffersons*. A lot of celebrities were there to raise money for AIDS. They were all to appear onstage together in the musical finale.

The event's producer walked up to Chauncey and said, "We're having all the soap stars, past and present, take the stage. You wanna come up?"

"Me?" Chauncey asked, flabbergasted.

"You were on *General Hospital* a few days, right?"

Chauncey nodded. Later he'd realize this producer, who worked a lot for ABC and *General Hospital*, was also a friend of PK's and knew this would be an event Chauncey would never forget.

So, there he was, on a stage packed with a hundred celebrities, before thousands in the Hollywood Bowl and millions watching on television. And he sang, or pretended to sing, "America the Beautiful." It was an unforgettable moment. One that took Chauncey far, far beyond his typical "who am I really" state.

After the song, they released scores of doves from each side of the stage. As they fluttered up toward the sunrise and the orchestra crescendoed, Chauncey felt it was the most beautiful scene he could imagine. It was spiritual. It was fantasy. It was Hollywood.

Yes, standing on stage with thousands giving them a standing ovation was quite a rush. He was always on the other side—in the audience, where his parents sat now. Now he was up here.

Sure, he knew the enthusiasm of those sitting in that amphitheater had nothing to do with him. But it was still a rush. And Chauncey would take it with him. He would see himself afterward on *Entertainment Tonight*.

Chauncey took a lot with him, hanging with soap stars. He began to realize this was a unique kind of belonging. And it constantly clashed with his more regular life at the Christian high school his parents wanted him to attend. He would qualify, during his senior year, as the student with the worst attendance record. His girlfriend came in second.

Everything was moved aside to fit his primary study course: life at *General Hospital*. Nothing could be scheduled on the weekends. So, Chauncey never attended any of the banquets, special events, senior trips. He signed up for home economics instead of auto mechanics, for example, because the former was scheduled in the afternoon, the latter first thing in the morning. And he just couldn't do early morning classes. Not after a night in Hollywood.

Chauncey had always hated school. People called him stupid. He had something like dyslexia. Spelling drove him crazy. It terrified him any time students had to read a chapter of some text aloud in class. Chauncey would count the people ahead of him, look down the number of paragraphs, and start practicing the one he'd be reading. He had to go over every word. "How to you pronounce that?" If he couldn't find the right paragraph, he'd go to the bathroom.

For Chauncey, cheating was something of a given. He was just trying to get by on the minimum.

One time, he had to pick up his sister, Charmaine, from the school's fall festival. He was so accustomed to life in that other Hollywood place, Chauncey didn't think about the beer can in his hand. The boys' dormitory dean spotted it. Chauncey tried to cover the can with his hat, but the man beckoned him over.

Chauncey shook his head and hurried the opposite way on the campus, crowded with parents and students. The dean gave chase; Chauncey threw the beer can into a bush. But he'd been spotted.

As a result, Chauncey was assigned to work duty every Sunday for two months. That senior year, he'd already been suspended for a week. Chauncey thought that a marvelous sentence. He could hang out with his *General Hospital* friends even more. But now he was supposed to scrape old paint off the white fence surrounding the corral where they taught horsemanship. Every weekend on campus? That just couldn't be. He was in a softball league with stars from *Happy Days*, *Laverne & Shirley*, *Mork & Mindy*. The games were on Sunday!

PK came to the rescue. She got a note from doctors who worked for the ABC network saying that he could not do paint scraping for medical reasons and that he was required to be with PK on Sundays.

These people were part of such big events. The American Music Awards. The Grammys. And someone would tell Chauncey, "Come on, you're going." Chauncey couldn't refuse.

At one professional soccer match, the *General Hospital* stars did the halftime show, playing a little soccer against personalities from a big LA radio station. Chauncey was asked to join them. So, there he was, sitting in the VIP lounge one summer day, then being escorted out on the field, looking around at fifty thousand fans in the LA Memorial Coliseum. This was the place where his dad had taken him to see Rams games. They'd be up in the nose-bleed section, looking through binoculars at these larger-than-life sports figures. And now he was running around on that same field for three minutes, doing his best to get a foot on the soccer ball.

He could talk to Skipper from *Gilligan's Island*, walking down Sunset Strip on the way to a benefit dinner at UCLA. Now he was Skipper's little buddy.

There was *Battle of the Network Stars*, charity events, marathons—and he could participate with the celebrities.

Finding Direction

This *General Hospital* life stressed out Chauncey's parents, of course. Marilyn worried about him drifting into the Hollywood lifestyle and away from his faith. There were confrontations early on. Once, Marilyn tried to put her foot down. Chauncey wanted to go away with PK and the *General Hospital* gang for a whole weekend.

Marilyn looked at her sixteen-year-old son and said, "You're way too young. You can't go." It didn't seem prudent to allow her boy to spend day and night with people who appeared to go against everything she believed in.

"Mom, I'm going."

"Chauncey, you can't!"

"Mom, I *am* going." Chauncey took the car keys and left. "I'll be back Monday morning."

How could he hang around the house when he could be at parties with the kind of people whose antics would appear the next day in all the soap magazines? And sometimes this kid would appear as well, standing beside so-and-so. It was only years later that Chauncey could begin to imagine the kind of stress he'd inflicted on his parents.

Chauncey graduated high school by the skin of his teeth. For years he would have nightmares about being back in school. But high school did teach him something important: what he wanted to do and what he didn't want to do. Chauncey knew he had the people skills to work in some capacity in the entertainment industry.

Chauncey and PK kept in touch over the years, even after the kid had to get a real job as an adult. And one day, she told him she'd become a Christian.

Chauncey wondered how.

She just started reading the Bible. Wanted to study what was really there. Nobody else could tell this woman where to go spiritually. She had to find the answers on her own. And when PK did run into Jesus, it was quite a collision. Her strong-willed nature became focused on growing as a believer.

Now she and Chauncey could talk about their challenges, their experiences as Christians. Sometimes he feared he was going in the opposite direction, drifting from his strict upbringing while she was getting some zeal for the Lord. But PK helped Chauncey

Marilyn: "He Was Meant to Go in a Different Direction"

I realized Chauncey is more of a risk taker than I am. His interests were in fields that I didn't understand—that whole Hollywood scene with the soap stars, for example. We expected him to get involved with all the church activities, go to a Christian college. It didn't happen. It was important for me that he earn a college degree; it wasn't important for him. Yes, I did worry a lot when he was sixteen or seventeen. When he'd call and say he'd be staying overnight with a bunch of Hollywood types, I almost panicked. He seemed way too young for that scene. Many times, I told him, "You have to come home. I want you home."

He'd just promise to be in school the next day. And he'd make it. But I still worried, of course. He didn't seem to have a goal in life that I recognized, wasn't working toward anything specific. And he started smoking. That was hard for me.

His personality type, the free spirit, is something I hadn't really seen up close. It just couldn't be found in our family history. You don't quite know what to do with it.

Now it's safe to say that the goals I had pictured so clearly for him weren't made exactly for him. He was meant to go in a different direction. And now I can see that's OK. He's done fine in his work.

And now I can be thankful that, even in that soap-star world, Chauncey always had someone who kind of looked out for him, took him under their wing, in a good way. Like makeup artist PK, who became a dedicated Christian during the time Chauncey hung out down there.

And when Chauncey graduated from high school, what do you know, a whole band of *General Hospital* people came up to congratulate him. That was pretty impressive.

appreciate the inspirational element of following Christ, like the music of Sandi Patty. PK became a big fan. And Chauncey had met her through his work for Christian television ministry.

Yes, those special tunes about Jesus helped him keep a grip on faith. And in time, Sandi and Chauncey would bond over adoption. She followed every step of his journey toward Loretta. Her husband Don had begun a similar trek in search of his biological parents. And the two of them had adopted a child. There was plenty to talk about. And through it all, there were plenty of beautiful songs Sandi Patty had made famous, which brought God into the picture.

And what Chauncey noticed was that God was still in the picture, rather brightly, even after PK was diagnosed with terminal cancer. She didn't want Chauncey to visit her in the hospital or on her deathbed. She wanted him to remember her as the beautiful, strong person he admired. But there was also acceptance. When the doctor showed PK X-rays that exposed telltale spots all over her body, revealing that the cancer had metastasized, she surprised him with the comment: "Those are God's fingerprints."

What PK meant was that she knew where she was going. And she believed she would see that kid she'd taken under her wing again in heaven.

The loss was devastating for Chauncey. It took him a long time to process the grief. But in working his way through it, he realized that he'd gotten an extra mom out of the blue. Yeah, this kid with the x factor, the hidden biological mother out there somewhere, out of touch, had received a celebrity mom who always looked out for him in her own way. Through PK, the kid who always lacked that sense of belonging had found a family among Hollywood's elite.

Meeting Lucy

And then Chauncey met Lucille Ball.

Even as a child, Chauncey had felt some connection with her. He watched *I Love Lucy* reruns every evening. It seemed he'd been looking at her from the time he was born, like that musical intro to the show was ringing in his ears even as a baby being held in his mother's arms after dinner.

The innocence and the laughter of this classic sitcom had a calming effect on Chauncey. He remembered being struck by the idea that the kid who played Little Ricky wasn't really their child, but they loved him anyway. And in the back of his mind, he always wondered why Fred and Ethel didn't have any kids.

Through junior high and high school, Chauncey would tell his friends that he was going to meet Lucille Ball one day. What were the chances? This little kid attending a church school in a small town? But he just knew it. They had some kind of connection.

Chauncey worked for twenty-five years in the entertainment business, and came close to meeting Lucille Ball several times. He'd be at some soap-star charity or celebrity award banquet and find that she'd just left. But he didn't get discouraged. It was going to happen.

One fateful evening, some people from ABC called, asking if he'd help put on a show to honor Ann-Margret and to raise money for Cedars-Sinai Medical Center. Chauncey happily agreed. Chauncey helped arrange for musical numbers, booked talent, put together a bio about Ann Margaret. What he didn't know was that one of the guests invited was Lucille Ball.

During the meet-and-greet time at the event, as celebrities walked through press lines, one of Chauncey's friends, Gwen, came up and whispered excitedly to Chauncey, "Look, there's Lucille Ball."

Chauncey was busy finding a better table for some personal friends of Ann-Margret. But he grabbed his friend and said, "Get your camera; I am not going to miss this opportunity."

Chauncey knew that a person just doesn't interrupt people while they're eating; it's essential to honor a celebrity's privacy. He noticed Lucille Ball was being led to her table. This was it— before the meal started. He followed her through the crowded ballroom. Chauncey had met and worked with many celebrities. She was "the one." She was the actress who'd essentially paved the way for all women in television and wrote the book on sitcoms. She was one of those few celebrities in the world who are known and loved by countless people, from five-year-olds to eighty-year-olds. She was more famous than presidents.

As Chauncey was approaching her table, he noticed Ann-Margret and Tom Bosley from *Happy Days* were walking over too. Since they were both participants in that night's program, the one he was working on, maybe that would make it easier to slip in.

Chauncey turned to Gwen and hissed, "Is there film in the camera? Makes sure it's focused right!" He was grabbing her hand so hard his fingernails almost drew blood. Years later, Gwen would still be teasing him about her "Lucille Ball scar."

Chauncey's mouth went dry. "What should I say?" he wondered. "'Excuse me, Miss Ball,' or, 'Pardon me, Lucy,' or, 'Oh Luuuucy,' like Desi did?" He was inches away.

Lucy looked up at Chauncey. His face must have been beaming like an angel's. "Excuse me, Miss Ball, but it would mean the world to me if I could have my photo taken with you."

She smiled politely. "Of course, but please kneel down here." Chauncey quickly realized if this star stood up, the whole room would have been hounding her for a picture.

So, he had to do it quickly. Chauncey knelt. Gwen took the picture.

Now Chauncey had to guard the camera with his life, never letting it out of his hands. Lucille Ball would depart before the lights came back up after the show.

He waited until 10:00 a.m. when the one-hour photo place opened. He was first in line and waited there the entire hour, hovering, wanting to make sure they didn't drop the film, or ruin it somehow, and praying his eyes had been open, praying it was in focus.

The photo came out. It would become Chauncey's best memory, an 8 × 10 photo on his wall.

Lucille Ball passed away not long after that little rendezvous.

Lucy and Ethel

Fast-forward several years to Bina trying to track down Chauncey's bio mom. Lucy and Ethel Marrison rang a bell. They were names from the *I Love Lucy* show, of course, something Chauncey talked about all the time. Well, why not check those out?

That proved to be the turning point. That was why Bina managed to zero in on an actual blood relative amid a hopelessly vast pool of possible connections. Lucy and Ethel would prove to be Loretta Marrison's aunts. They would lead Bina to the happy ending.

And they were quite involved in the adoption story. Loretta came out to California to have her baby because her Aunt Ethel lived in the San Fernando Valley. Ethel took care of her in the weeks before delivery.

Sometime later, Aunt Ethel began feeling guilty. (That emotion spreads pretty widely in the world of adoption.) Why didn't she adopt that baby, keep him in the family?

While she was in the hospital, helping Loretta through the birth process, Ethel had overheard the adoptive parents talking about their home in Burbank. Ethel found herself driving around the Burbank suburbs, keeping an eye out for a little redheaded boy. Red hair was a trait of Loretta's. Wouldn't it be nice to catch a glimpse of this little kid, playing happily in the yard with his adoptive parents?

When Chuck and Marilyn were bringing their new son home from the hospital, they stopped at a restaurant called The Bear Pit to grab a bite. Years later, it would become one of Chauncey's favorite restaurants, and he actually talked with a waitress there who remembered the Smith couple bringing in that newborn.

Well, The Bear Pit was one of Aunt Ethel's favorite restaurants too. Maybe they ate there together several times without knowing it.

Something to Know: Picking Up Providences

These little details wouldn't qualify in most people's minds as a miracle. If you're a skeptical person, there's nothing in this story that's going to force you to believe in a God of providences.

But for Chauncey, it all proved to be a meaningful sign. It seemed that a heavenly Father indeed appeared in the details. Chauncey wasn't just out there flailing around for an identity by himself. His perspective was: "What are the chances of my finding my bio mom? What are the chances of my running into Lucille Ball?"

Someone significant had made those things happen.

Many adopted kids don't automatically grow up with a benign picture of a Father in heaven. Their father on earth may be quite a stretch to picture. He may be a no-show. And so it takes a bit more work to develop a trust in someone "up there" who can provide for our needs; it takes effort to get a grip on divine providences.

But Chauncey's experience is one example of the effort being well worth it. Sometimes it's a matter of choosing a certain perspective. You simply open yourself to the possibility that things can work together for good. And sometimes keeping an eye out for providences seems to multiply them. The more you acknowledge that some positive event trickled down from God, the more such events you experience.

> *The more you acknowledge that some positive event trickled down from God, the more such events you experience.*

And this can be especially heartwarming for adopted individuals. After all, they didn't drop into a world of Mom and apple pie, rosebuds and butterflies. They came into a world where blood didn't prove thicker than circumstances. So, they've often got a built-in doubt about things going well for them. And people like PK, who can talk about God's fingerprints in the worst of circumstances, are a definite inspiration.

Chauncey's buddy, Greg, had a rather dark take on the world, despite being raised by godly, nurturing adoptive parents. He liked to party; he could have a good time (especially after several drinks). But something kept him from believing that the unknown of his biological past might yield something good. He couldn't take that step out there; he couldn't pray his way toward solving a mystery.

The sad thing is Greg often showed signs of really wanting to seek God. Sometimes, he'd read the Bible as if on a genuine quest for answers. But that providential Word just didn't connect enough with him to send him out in search of providences in the present.

Chauncey, on the other hand, did read the Bible. And when adopted people can begin picking up on providences, on little signs that there's a Father out there with their interests at heart and who can fill some holes inside.

Chauncey's experience, and those of countless other people, tells adopted individuals that looking for providences can be very meaningful. Praying for them can bring recognizable results. In your journey toward that biological parent, don't just stare down at the sidewalk. Take a gander at what's happening around you. You just might make out a reassuring nudge from heaven.

Chapter 6
Chauncey

Chauncey found himself pacing in his condo with one thought going over and over in his head, like something you can't stop stuttering. "It's her; it's her; it's her."

All those years of wondering. What if she's not even alive anymore? What if she doesn't want to talk? What if I'm not anything like this birth mother?

What if she's not even alive anymore? What if she doesn't want to talk? What if I'm not anything like this birth mother?

Now the answer was waiting on the other end of a phone line. He paced from living room to bedroom and back again, fumbling with the white cordless phone. He couldn't sit. He couldn't stand still. He couldn't do anything.

Chauncey practiced dialing the number a couple of times, then hung up. It just seemed far too big a task for him. Like breaking the sound barrier. He simply didn't have the engine to break through, break through these decades of mystery, these family histories, this first big one-on-one. So, he began praying, "Lord, please help dial the number."

It wasn't a frivolous prayer. And looking back much later, Chauncey got the impression that it was like God had dialed the number for him. Strength, determination, *something* came from somewhere else. Because as he stood there nervously staring at that stupid phone, a voice said, "Hello."

Right away it was Loretta apologizing. "I'm so sorry for not telling Bina right away it was me. I was in shock. I have four daughters that I need to tell—today."

Their first conversation would be an emotional blur. But one thing, one sentence, kept wanting to come out of Chauncey: "Thank you so much for choosing life."

And he wanted pictures, family pictures. "Can you send me some?"

"Oh, yes, of course."

"Welcome, Chauncey"

When Chauncey stepped off the plane in Columbus that day, when the blur turned into tunnel vision as he caught Loretta Martin's face, it was nothing but tears all around. Mom tears. Son tears. Sister tears. At least he thought these women standing there must be his half-sisters. The whole airport seemed to be crying.

Then it suddenly turned into smiles and laughter. Chauncey couldn't keep the joy from bubbling up. This was like winning the Super Bowl. Cameras kept flashing. Strangers were applauding.

Chauncey was introduced to Loretta's husband, then to two of his four half-sisters. A lot was going on. But, really, it was all about her face.

As they walked through the airport, Loretta and Chauncey kept staring at each other with a hunger that few people in the world can understand. Between the expressions of awe, the phrases about how surreal it all seemed— "I can't believe you're here; I'm here"—these two people were poring over features, gestures, expressions. And they were picking up clues by the basketful. So *that's* who I am! They'd instantly become students of each other. Little things clicked in split seconds and got tucked away in the back of their heads. Recognition, resonance, revelation—they piled up as they waited for baggage, as they rode in the back-seat hand in hand.

Yes, there was some small talk. How the trip went. How nerve-wracking it had all been. All the anticipation. But above all, they kept studying each other.

On arriving in the Cleveland suburb of Conneaut, at the home of Loretta's daughter, Sue, where they'd be staying, Chauncey saw a huge sign stretched across the front porch: "Welcome, Chauncey." It had been signed by scores of people.

Inside, what had been an overwhelming greeting at the airport turned into something far larger than life (or, at least, larger than any life Chauncey could grasp). He was hugging the other two of his four half-sisters, shaking hands with cousins, nephews, aunts—was the whole town of Conneaut here? —hearing name after name tossed at him.

Chauncey spoke the appropriate greetings. But he could hardly feel his body. He couldn't tell if he was walking around this crowded living room or somehow floating. There was his name on a big cake. He blew out some candles. And the scene faded.

Chauncey didn't catch his breath until after Loretta drove him back to his hotel. He'd explained that he would need a little time alone to decompress, to absorb it all. Fortunately, she understood.

And, yes, he needed it desperately. Chauncey called his parents, Bina, and a few friends just so he could debrief, get out something of what had just happened. Maybe it would begin to register. It wasn't easy getting hold of something that had been building inside him, one anxious moment or question or hope at a time, for thirty-five years.

The next morning, Loretta and Chauncey managed a nice, quiet breakfast together. But then, back at the house in the evening, there was another big celebration. Even more relatives. Aunt

Carol had brought over her clan. So many welcomes. So many open arms. People who hadn't even known he existed days before. It was wonderful. But it also threw him out of his body again. And Chauncey realized something rather odd. *General Hospital* was coming to his rescue in a way. Chauncey had studied acting for a time back then, encouraged by his Hollywood friends to consider a career in their world. And now those basic techniques proved quite helpful, because inside he was just about to lose it. But he could concentrate on the motions, the gestures, the expressions that fit the moment. He could focus on action and response. And it worked.

He had to play a role there: Newly Discovered Adopted Son. It was a role he'd never played before, never imagined playing. Everyone in that room knew everyone else. Except him. Everyone had all kinds of anecdotes to throw around. Except him. "I'm like the ugly duckling or something—and this party's about me," Chauncey thought.

Chauncey couldn't just express his feelings. That would send him to some back room, curled up in a little ball. He had to be the person for whom these people were looking. But yes, Hollywood carried him along that night. Sure, he could stretch his way into that role. He could exclaim back; he could laugh with them; he could open his arms too.

Hellos and Good-Byes

Later, lying there in his hotel room alone, trying to take it all in, Chauncey remembered scenes on television that really got to him. Talk shows would sometimes feature people reunited with their families, parents they hadn't seen in years. And he would start bawling. Even as a teenager, even as a young man, he wasn't accustomed to this. But the tears flooded out.

Chauncey remembered how something had hit him, quite unexpectedly as a kid, while watching nature shows on TV. There was an episode about Mama Pig dying and leaving a little piglet to wander around in the barn. But a dog came sniffing around and ended up nursing Little Piggy. Yeah, the little creature was nudging Mama Dog's stomach, lapping up the milk, but Chauncey could tell these were two different species. He could tell which animals belong together and which don't. A puppy can swim, a piglet can't. A puppy barks, a piglet snorts.

And that odd scene stuck with Chauncey. Maybe that was the niche he occupied in the world. He was fed and nurtured. But really belonging? That was another story.

And now, years later, Chauncey realized all the more why those scenes had resonated inside him.

There had been a lot of numbing in his life. Forgetting you're adopted can be a good thing. It gives you a reasonably normal life. But there were strong feelings that wanted to surge up at odd times that Chauncey just tried to ignore. He didn't understand where they were coming from. He didn't want to harbor them.

But now it was all coming together. *"So this is who I am!"* All that hidden stuff inside was now spread out, bouncing around among family members filling a living room in Ohio, talking and gesturing, giving pieces of himself plenty of space to be expressed.

What's more, as Chauncey and Loretta talked, they began to realize they'd both probably seen those same talk shows about the adopted children meeting their birth parents. And both had told themselves, subconsciously, this would never happen to them. They suppressed the possibility. It was someone else's story. But still, there were the same intense emotions. Yes, the same tears, at the same time, on both coasts. Chauncey in California, Loretta in North Carolina.

Later, reflecting in the middle of the night on this great big hello and all that it meant to him, Chauncey would remember a big good-bye he had to say. And he would see more clearly why good-byes and hellos often take on a larger-than-life feel for adopted people.

It was about his other sister, Charmaine. They called her Char. Some would refer to her as his "real" younger sister, the one he grew up with, also adopted by Chuck and Marilyn.

Char was moving to New York. She'd met a guy out there and was going to marry him. He seemed scary to the family. But Char was an adult now and the divorced mother of two children. She had to live her own life.

After her divorce, Char and her daughter and son, April and Tarren, moved back in with Chuck and Marilyn. Chauncey still lived at home and took his role as uncle very seriously. They all took roles in raising the kids.

Chauncey knew that his sister had always struggled with the fact of adoption. Her fears seemed even bigger. There were many nights where she'd been afraid to sleep in the dark. During down days, she'd say things like, "I wish I'd never been adopted. I wish I'd never been born."

And yes, when teenage conflicts flared up with Mom and Dad, she'd sometimes throw out the "you don't love me" line that adopted kids always have in their arsenal.

But Char tried her best as a mother. And Chauncey made sure he was in April's and Tarren's lives from the time they were infants. He attended all their school events, sometimes took them to church. He had pictures, all the way from preschool graduation to high school graduation. There were memorable trips together to Disneyland and Magic Mountain and Las Vegas.

The kids' father wasn't very involved in their lives. So yes, Chauncey felt quite a bit like a dad. Maybe even a strict dad. When they'd go out for a fast-food treat, Chauncey would let them order their drink, cheeseburger, and fries, but then say, "OK, you can have something sweet, but you need to finish whatever you ordered first." At home, he'd often hold the ice cream until they'd eaten their greens. When handing over a little birthday money, he'd say, "Have fun, kids, and please try to save some of it."

Chauncey understood their individual personalities as they blossomed through childhood. April was the peacemaker, the caregiver; she wanted everyone to get along. Even as a little girl, she had an instinct for balancing out the extremes or the quirks of others. April always had the biggest smile in the room.

Tarren, a couple of years younger, was the quiet, reserved kid. A lot was going on in his head. Sometimes Chauncey sensed he had been deeply wounded by the absence of a father. Even the best of uncles and grandparents don't take the place of an actual dad.

Still, these two, Chauncey realized, were nothing like him. He'd been a pretty bratty kid growing up. He loved his parents, sure, but he was always pushing the rules, tiptoeing around boundaries. April and Tarren actually listened when Chauncey gave them warnings or advice! And they were fun to be with.

This father role was a big experience for Chauncey. In his early thirties, he realized he'd take a bullet for April and Tarren. This was the first time he truly felt, in the gut, the love someone could feel for a child. It was a different sensation, a different experience. Not like the crazy love you could fall into with a girlfriend. Not like the love you might feel over time for a good buddy. Not even the deep love you felt for nurturing parents. This kind of devotion had its own kind of pull, its own kind of weight.

And then came the big move to New York. Char wanted to start a new life with this guy. She drove across the country to settle in with him. Marilyn and Chuck were going to fly April and Tarren, now fifteen and twelve, out a little later in the summer after they'd finished their school year.

The night before April and Tarren were to leave, Chauncey found himself crying a lot in his condo. This departure was getting to him. He was a young man. He had piles of friends. He could party with the best of them. But this unique love for children started shaking him up.

Chauncey knew, of course, it was best for April and Tarren to be with their mother. But it wasn't easy, this good-bye.

In the morning, he drove over to his parents' house and hugged April a lot. She could express her feelings more easily. They exchanged plenty of "I love you's" and "I'll miss you's." He hugged Tarren too, of course, and said the same things. But he was trying to be the strong one and avoided Chauncey's gaze after a while.

Driving back home, Chauncey still couldn't stop the tears. He knew he couldn't take seeing them off at the airport. Good-byes and airports had always been way too intense for him. But this was a whole new kind of separation.

Back in his condo, Chauncey went to bed, feeling like he'd been kicked in the stomach. He started a twenty-four-hour pity party, thinking about those two kids clear across the country, thinking about how frail "I'll see you soon" now sounded. It was like grieving a death. The saddest good-bye ever.

Chauncey tried to tell himself this good-bye wasn't about him. It was about kids being with their mother. But he couldn't escape that "why does everyone leave me" emotion shoving things around inside him.

Yeah, good-byes are brutal.

April Kearns: "Adoption Has Blessed Us"

Adoption affects the 2nd and 3rd generation: There will always be "the one that was adopted...." Since my mom, brother, and I lived with my grandparents for a while they were such a huge part of my life. I too recall when people, even family members, that knew my mom was adopted, would say how much I looked like my grandmother. As a young child, I just loved hearing that, but as I got older and understood adoption I realized there was no way I could look like my grandmother. Being the 2nd generation we too are the ones that aren't blood related at the family events. We are also the ones that don't look like Aunt Bonnie or Uncle Bill. If I have children, I look forward to the talk about our wonderful family and how much adoption has blessed us.

Something to Know: Hellos and Good-Byes

Transitions that most people take in stride often take on more weight for adopted individuals. Every good-bye has a bit of an edge to it. Somewhere deep inside, there's that connection to the original good-bye, the good-bye that set the course of their lives, the good-bye that a birth parent made to an infant.

Every good-bye has a bit of an edge to it.

People who've always had good bonds with the birth parents who raised them have a hard time imagining what it's really like. Many people even get a kick out of transitions; they enjoy the adventure of good-bye.

But for those who have a birth parent somewhere hidden from them, waving a hand as someone departs is never a simple thing. Little separations typically make them feel a little shaky. Big good-byes can pull the ground out from under them.

So, it helps to understand the journey of the adopted toward a birth parent in terms of good-byes and hellos. The hello they're reaching out for can have such a huge resonance in their lives because good-byes have always reverberated so deeply. The meeting with a face resembling their own can feel like such big closure because every face that disappears reminds them of the faces they've never seen.

And this is why many adopted individuals never take that journey. They're afraid the hoped-for hello will turn into just another good-bye. That the birth parent may not want contact. That they may even freak out at the sight of their child. And the adopted one often just can't imagine enduring the big good-bye that climaxes all the other painful good-byes in their life.

You can't force anyone to take that journey. You can't determine how someone else is going to find closure. Everybody has to ultimately make their own decisions about hello and good-bye. But people like Chauncey feel very strongly that the journey is worth it, whatever the outcome. Yes, it's scary. Yes, it's intimidating. But there can be such healing in the end. There *is* a kind of closure, even if you don't end up establishing a relationship with a birth parent.

It's just not worth running from this possibility. It will always haunt you. It will always take a toll. And often you can establish relationships with other blood relatives, even if the birth parents are still emotionally unavailable. There are people out there, almost in every instance, with whom you

There are people out there, almost in every instance, with whom you can bond.

can bond. You'll get something out of the journey. You may even find yourself in a room full of people who are complete strangers but who keep expressing their love, who keep saying how happy they are to have found you.

So, Chauncey encourages the adopted this way: Just step into it. There's a part of you that just has to find out. Take the jump and see what happens.

He could say that especially because of something Loretta had said on his birthday, the first birthday they'd been able to speak together. She told him, "I feel like sending you thirty-five birthday cards. I wanted to send you one every year of your life. Now, every October 1, I can send you a real birthday card, instead of a make-believe one in my mind. That's what I've always done."

Rita, Chauncey, Loretta, Sue, Leigh Ann and Shelly.

Chapter 7
Sisters

Rita had grown up with three younger sisters. They had the usual girl stuff going on, but without much of the jealousy or hissy fits that sometimes accompany that much estrogen in a house. She and her sisters had sometimes tried to imagine what it would be like having a brother; there were plenty of pros and cons. But it had always seemed intriguing. It was only when they started venturing into boyfriends that this other side of the world—male peers—came close. And even then, it was only a special-event kind of thing.

But now she found herself talking on the phone with a brother out of the blue. Chauncey Smith, flesh-and-blood related. Same mother. Now the oldest sibling in the family.

But what really surprised Rita was how much Chauncey seemed like someone familiar, not someone she had just started talking to in midlife.

The Marrison family always had a worrywart streak. And Chauncey showed the same bursts of anxiety about first-time meetings and work deadlines. She liked his sense of humor, his warmth, his talkativeness.

When he flew out to visit and they were having coffee on the back patio one day, she observed that he had that same Marrison skin color too—light and a little freckled. Everyone had it except their youngest sister, Sue.

"Yeah, you have the same freckles I do," Chauncey observed.

They could definitely see that.

Sisters

It had all started for Rita when Loretta asked her to come over that afternoon and broke the news that she had a brother.

After Loretta made contact, Rita would be the first of the sisters to make a call.

She left a message. "Hi, this is your sister Rita from North Carolina. Just wanted to talk. Welcome to the family. We're excited to know we have a brother."

That would be something quite remarkable for Chauncey, because an hour later he had a message from someone named Shelly. Oh, another sister. "I can't believe I have a brother who lives in California!" she exclaimed.

Within twenty-four hours, Chauncey had talked with all four of his half-sisters. Everyone was welcoming. And he'd even chatted with Richard, their father.

Chauncey called Rita back first, and it felt pretty exciting for her. Here was a person to get to know, in the middle of your life, who could be called brother after all those years of pure sisterhood.

The Marrison family was pretty big and pretty close. There were a lot of male cousins, good guys, she and her sisters had sometimes hung out with. But still, this was different. This was someone who came out of the same womb.

Rita told him her first child was a boy, Loretta's first grandchild. And she could well imagine what it must have been like for her mother to hold that baby boy—and never be able to hold her own for years afterward.

When Chauncey flew out for the big face-to-face meeting with Loretta, the first thing Rita remembered thinking was how much he looked like their mother. All four sisters had made a big banner out in front of Sue's house in Ohio when he came in with Loretta from the airport. "Welcome, Chauncey."

And that first hug wasn't like hugging a stranger at all. Chauncey looked handsome and confident, didn't seem uncomfortable or nervous. But yes, he was very observant, checking out all the faces there. Where exactly did he fit in biologically? It was fun and edgy. They'd just dug up someone from the distant past and he was very alive and he was displaying these gestures that kept ringing bells.

During subsequent visits, Rita began to see more and more how she and Chauncey looked and acted the same. More recognition. Her gestures and facial expressions were reflected in this newly discovered brother. Chauncey loved learning that he and Shelly enjoyed naps and Sister Sue loved to ride horses, just like he did.

The two or three days they spent together never seemed quite long enough.

Chauncey's second oldest sister, Leigh Anne, had a very similar experience. She accompanied her mother to the airport for the big meeting. Chauncey was a lot taller than she thought. After all the hugs and tears, Leigh Anne noted how much Chauncey and Loretta enjoyed taking each other in. She took a picture that she still carries in her wallet. Yes, the resemblance as they stood side by side was uncanny.

Everyone had always told Leigh Anne how much she looked like her mother. They said that to Rita too. Now there was someone else to share in the likeness.

Months before, when Chauncey first called her, Leigh Anne had the flu. His humor struck her right away. They quickly asked each other a lot of questions, found out things they had in common, and after the conversation, this sister felt her flu fading.

Then, after the big meeting, on their first weekend together, the sisters took Chauncey around to places where they grew up, houses where they were little girls, schools they'd attended. And they looked out on Lake Erie, taking in the view with a brother who now seemed suddenly very much a part of the family. And Leigh Anne felt a little pang: What would it have been like to grow up with this man? There were so many memories of childhood she could share with her three sisters. But with Chauncey, well, they had to start making them now.

It was fun telling all her friends she had a brother now. All the sisters showed photos of Chauncey to their friends to prove he really did exist. Photo albums had taken on a new meaning for them. Chauncey would sit down between them and look over their years and their relatives, often asking, "Who's that?" There was a lot of explaining to do about this cousin, that aunt. And now Chauncey got a taste of all that he had missed: a whole lot of family, a lot of happy times together.

Chauncey couldn't help prattling on to the whole family about the impact of these photos. He was looking through a family history, feeling like he was a part of it, like he belonged there. But he hadn't been there for most of it. And then, all of a sudden, there's Chauncey, popping up in the last pages of the family albums. He smiled when he realized that people would wonder, "Where did *he* come from?"

That was another thing that struck Chauncey during these encounters with the Marrisons. The unspoken assumption, as you begin this journey toward your bio mom, is that you will run into the Big Answer. You'll see the face. This is where you came from. This is what your biological mother is like. And that brings satisfaction. You solve the mystery.

There is indeed a great deal of satisfaction, but what's interesting is that the mystery only increases. Now you know more. But now you know a lot less too. There are all these new people around you, people with all kinds of lives stretching back in time, people who are related to you in some way. And you know so little about them.

It's a little like getting married. The big event is what matters. You make the ultimate connection. But then there's this whole other family to get in sync with, say, over the holidays. There's a lot to learn—and always a lot to feel. While watching Loretta's grandkids, nephews, and nieces play with a bunch of adult relatives, Chauncey imagined himself there, as a kid, playing with Loretta. He was observing all these little ones going to Grandma, excitedly showing her things or asking her questions, and Loretta delighting in them. Chauncey imagined himself into the scene. That could have been him.

Chauncey's sisters also noticed the look Loretta would get as she observed them interacting with him. Seeing Chauncey laughing with her daughters, even teasing them about stuff, seeing him play with their kids—it was a joy almost too big to handle.

And that old guilt would spring up too. Loretta couldn't help it. Chauncey and her girls had never been able to play together as kids. They hadn't teased each other or helped each other out growing up. Loretta couldn't get over the fact that after all these years, her five kids were together. As happy as she was, she also felt bad that they had all missed all those years as children.

Chauncey always tried to smile away any signs of bio mom guilt. He knew he couldn't make it just disappear. But there *was* something Chauncey discovered in this whole process of acquiring sisters. He could help Bio Mom a little. He could give something back.

In one of their long conversations, Loretta confessed the distress she'd felt over one of her daughters who just didn't slip into the standard sexual orientation of the others.

She had a very hard time accepting that. She felt she'd failed this girl somehow. Maybe she didn't love her enough. Maybe she didn't hug her enough. Why did she have this issue, while the other daughters didn't at all?

In looking into her teary eyes, Chauncey could tell Loretta had beaten herself up for years about this. Chauncey said a quick prayer, looked her squarely in the face, and said with conviction, "This has nothing to do with you, Loretta—with how you treated her. I was raised by the most loving parents in the world, and I've struggled with some of those same issues." He also told her about research he'd ran across that showed adopted people tend to have a higher level of sexuality, which includes sexual adventurousness. For some, sexual identity is not a simple, settled thing. A lot of stuff in their lives isn't. But he ended it by telling her firmly that both he and Leigh Anne had been raised by totally different parents in totally different places. And look at this remarkable similarity. It wasn't about upbringing; it was more likely a tendency somewhere in the genes they had in common.

He would always remember the look on her face. Such relief and gratitude. That was quite a rush for Chauncey. Being able to help Bio Mom get through something? Wow, where did that come from?

And then Loretta gave back. She found out that Chauncey had never told his parents about his sexual adventures and misadventures. He didn't want to hurt them. He didn't want them to blame themselves for any of it.

But Loretta looked him in the face and said, "You need to be honest with your parents. I guarantee they will accept you unconditionally. I know a mother's love overshadows everything else." She also told him that the biggest regret a parent has is not knowing about something deep, something life-changing in a child.

Within a day Chauncey had blurted everything out to Dad. Well, almost everything. He confessed some of the wild things he'd done, after all, it was the time of sex, drugs, and rock-n-roll. He said he wanted him and Mom to know these were his choices. This was about him—good or bad—not about them.

Chuck gave him a big hug.

Chauncey asked him to help with the disclosure to Marilyn. There's always something bigger about telling Mom.

Not long afterward, Marilyn came to her son, teary-eyed, and asked, "Why would you be afraid to tell me?"

"I just didn't want to stress you out or worry you, Mom."

More hugs. More assurances of unconditional love.

Finding Suzanne

Chauncey's interaction with his new family, and with his new half-sisters in particular, made him think with a pang about his sister Charmaine, also adopted by Chuck and Marilyn. She had her struggles too. Sometimes it seemed that old abandonment thing was a shadow hanging over her every day.

After Chauncey's wonderful experience with Loretta, he very much wanted Charmaine to find her own bio mom. Bina, again, was happy to get on the Internet to track the woman down.

She came up with a woman named Suzanne, who lived in Victorville, just north of Los Angeles in the high desert. A bit of paperwork uncovered showed that Charmaine had been born Simone, and was in foster care for a few weeks.

Bina even came up with an address. But what was the best way to make contact? They were having a hard time getting through on the phone.

So, Chauncey suggested Char write her mom a letter. She tried to be as nonthreatening as possible: "I'm alive and OK. You have two wonderful grandkids."

Chauncey drove up to Victorville with that letter (addressed with "To Suzanne from Simone") attached to a balloon and flowers. He wanted to look like he was delivering a happy greeting.

Walking up to the house, he didn't know if this woman was going to cry for joy, faint, or slam the door in his face

The woman who responded to his knock didn't look like a very happy person.

"Are you Suzanne?" Chauncey smiled.

"Yes."

"I have a delivery here from Simone." He handed her the message—with its friendly attachments.

"Oh. Thank you," she said, rather emotionless.

And so Chauncey left, saying simply, "Have a nice day."

Months passed with no response. Finally, Charmaine received a letter from Suzanne's therapist. It stated, very formally, that Suzanne didn't want any contact. Her pregnancy was the result of a rape. There weren't many good memories associated with the whole experience. Suzanne had been in therapy for decades.

Upon hearing this, Chauncey flashed back to his little sister's reactions to the word "rape" over the years. It always seemed to spark a fear in her that a little girl, growing up in a sheltering Christian home, shouldn't have. Even before she was old enough to know what rape was, she was horrified by it. Come to find out, her bio mother was raped. Chauncey believed his sister inherited that fear.

Chauncey also reflected on his sister's fears of being alone. And he felt terribly sad that she still would be, in a sense. No contact with her bio mom. No happy ending.

It was especially difficult for Marilyn to see her daughter have an ending as bad as Chauncey's had been good. Who would want to reject her child—again?

The words of explanation in the letter from Charmaine's bio mom struck Marilyn as cruel and awful: "If it wasn't for my therapist, I couldn't write at all."

Who would say that?

Now she knew her daughter's genesis had been a brutal rape. But wait. The letter also said she'd been married to the birth father at the time. So, what did that mean?

After thirty-two years of therapy and she still couldn't handle this connection? This was the hardest thing for Marilyn to deal with. And she just couldn't make it up to her precious only daughter. The only way she could try to comfort herself and Charmaine was to say that it was better to know something than nothing. After all, that's what Chauncey had said.

Something to Know: The Essential Element

The meeting of these sisters and their brother highlights perhaps the most essential element of this whole journey to find your biological parent. It's something that's perhaps so obvious we often overlook it: love.

The amount of love people receive determines how this whole experience will turn out far more than any other factor. Geography is minor. Lifestyles aren't a big deal. The path to the rendezvous can vary greatly. But what's in the heart—that determines everything.

Chauncey was very fortunate to have been raised by loving, nurturing parents. The four sisters were blessed by a loving, nurturing mother and father. That shaped them more than anything else. And so this discovery of a new brother, this discovery of four sisters Chauncey didn't even know existed—it didn't threaten them at all. It didn't touch some hidden insecurity and make it jump out through all kinds of emotions.

Unfortunately, Char's bio mom had lifelong struggles with this issue of love and intimacy. She just couldn't seem to get over the rape or other misfortunes in her life. She remained trapped by them. Love just couldn't break through.

The basic truth is this: If you're loved, you stretch. If you're not, everything's a threat.

> *If you're loved, you stretch. If you're not, everything's a threat.*

Rita, Leigh Anne, Shelly, and Sue were intrigued by this human being that mirrored them in various ways. They enjoyed the novelty of suddenly having a brother. They even liked to show him off to friends sometimes.

Chauncey, even though sometimes overwhelmed by this new family and all they brought to him, found the whole process very rewarding. It was delightful getting to know each member of his new family.

That's how it goes when people are loved. They are prepared to stretch out in life and absorb new experiences. They are prepared to grow.

There was one moment in particular when Chauncey felt love hit him in the chest. It happened on his very first visit to the Marrisons. Walking in Loretta's house down a hallway, he glanced over and saw pictures on the wall. The four daughters' high school graduation pictures proudly displayed there. And one more. Chauncey Smith's graduation picture too. The one Marilyn had sent.

Chapter 8

No Dad

Flying to Cleveland, Chauncey looked out the window at thirty-three thousand feet and wondered how he was going to pull this off. If his emotions had been intense on the journey to meet Bio Mom, they were going to be even edgier crashing this wedding. What was it going to be like, meeting his blood relatives—anonymously?

After all, Loretta had wanted contact. She knew Chauncey was coming to see her. He knew there'd be a big welcome for him. But these people had politely declined any contact or correspondence.

Ray

It all started a few years after Chauncey and Loretta's reconnection. That had gone so well that Chauncey felt eager to contact his biological father. Loretta had a name, Ray, and a city, Cleveland. She hadn't seen or heard from the man since before Chauncey's birth.

But Bina, playing Sherlock Holmes again, managed to track him down. She got Ray on the phone, starting with her usual story about researching a family tree. Then she zeroed in on the real news.

"Do you know Loretta Marrison?"

"Uh, yeah, I remember her."

"Did you know she was pregnant?"

"Yeah, I heard about that through the grapevine over the years. She had a baby girl."

"Well, she's had four daughters. But before the girls, there was a baby boy."

Ray gave a little unbothered chuckle, "What do ya know?"

"You have a son."

Bina quickly added the disclaimers. Chauncey didn't want anything from him. He's fine, doing well in life. But Bina could hear a woman's distressed voice in the background asking, "What? Who?"

Ray started to explain to the woman, "Well, I've got a son. Honey, you knew about this."

"No, I didn't!"

Screaming in the background continued.

So, Ray had to tell Bina, "Now's not a good time; let me get back to you."

"Sure. All Chauncey wants is just pictures. You know, for his memories."

A day later, Ray called back. His wife, Betty, was not taking this well. She didn't want any contact. And they didn't want to have to tell their kids about this other child. Ray was cool about it, apologetic. He didn't wish Chauncey ill at all, but…

Bina tried a couple of times to get hold of Ray again. But the wife always answered the phone, so Bina hung up. Had she banned her husband from the phone?

After Chauncey heard what happened, he mulled it over for days. Just what was going on in his father's household? A clear picture emerged. Betty was it. She was in control of everything. And she was the villain.

It gave Chauncey a way to blame someone besides his father for this tubing out from any contact. Yeah, that was it—all these years, that woman wouldn't let him get anywhere near the past.

A few months later, something happened that seemed to Chauncey a godsend. One morning, Chauncey's half-sister Sue, who lived near Cleveland at the time, was having a cup of coffee and looking through the newspaper. She happened on a wedding announcement: the daughter of Ray Campbell was getting married. The name rang a bell. Yes, on one of Chauncey's visits, she'd overheard them talking about this Ray guy, Mom's first boyfriend of thirty-five years ago.

Sue looked at the address in the paper. All this time had she been living forty-five minutes from her brother's dad? Could it be the same man?

Sue called Chauncey up and asked if he had a picture of this Campbell sister.

"No, I have no idea what she looks like."

"Well, I have one."

Sue clipped out the wedding announcement and mailed it to Chauncey.

There she was, beaming with her fiancé. And there was a date and time for the event. That started Chauncey thinking.

Later, Chauncey would realize that his animosity toward Ray's wife had fueled the idea for the trip too. "How dare she!" he'd thought. "I don't owe her anything. What is she anyway, my half sibling's parent? Making contact is the best revenge!"

Wedding Crashers

Chauncey brought a friend named Craig along on the trip to Cleveland. He was there for moral support and for pictures. Chauncey wanted video shot at the wedding, and he wanted to be in the video, standing next to these family members, shaking hands as an anonymous guest. He wasn't going to identify himself. He didn't want to cause a scene and ruin his half sister's wedding day. She had to be the center of the event.

Even if people got suspicious, Chauncey would admit nothing. He would stay anonymous.

A few hours before the ceremony, Chauncey and Craig drove by their home address to check out the scene. This could have been his childhood home. This could have been his life.

As their rental car cruised by, Chauncey felt an instant sense of thanksgiving. The neighborhood just wasn't *him*. A very small-town feel, with brown grass and sagging fences. Industries in the area likely going downhill. Most people probably never left.

They checked the video camera fifteen times to make sure it worked. There was no way Chauncey wasn't going to get a record of this. They checked their two still cameras. He was going to get a picture of himself, standing beside his father, his half-brother, and his two half-sisters. He would have their faces, period. He'd know exactly what they looked like. And who he resembled most. How can anyone not want to know how much he looks like his father? So much in his bio mom and Marrison sisters had jumped out at him.

Craig and Chauncey also carefully went over their options, plans A, B, and C—what they would do if someone asked who they were, what they would do if they had to leave early.

They hurriedly took seats in the Catholic church just before the ceremony started, sitting on the bride's side. Chauncey looked over the program and glanced around at the hundred people there, wondering who he was related to.

The first person to come down the aisle was the mother of the bride. Chauncey refrained from saying aloud the descriptions of her that came to mind. She was escorted by her son, the program said. Yes, that would be the half-brother. Video tape that—there he is, walking by.

The matron of honor slowly walked by to music. A half-sister. Chauncey held the video camera up close to his face as Craig took stills. He was worried someone might recognize him as a blood relative and cause trouble. What if Ray looked at him, and he just knew this was his son. It could ruin the whole wedding.

The bridal music began, and everyone stood to their feet. Chauncey knew that as soon as he turned around he'd be facing his father and half-sister. Nervously, he looked. There they were, walking slowly past the guests. Chauncey almost lost it; he blinked at the camera lens, tearing up. Craig had to take the video camera as Chauncey almost lost it. Fortunately, every eye was on the bride. Chauncey could stare at his half-sister and father without fear of exposure.

Few similarities jumped out to Chauncey. Nothing like what he'd seen in Loretta.

As the ceremony began, Chauncey noticed that other guests would tiptoe up the side aisles to get better camera angles. So, he and Craig joined them at times. Chauncey wanted all the visual information he could get.

Afterward, as the bridal party said hello to the guests, Chauncey knew the moment had come. It was nerve-wracking, but he had to get a picture with them.

He noticed the matron of honor, his half-sister, standing just outside the church, smoking with some of the bridesmaids. So, Chauncey walked up while Craig videotaped and asked, "Could you give me directions to the reception?"

Done. One down, two to go.

Next, Chauncey approached his half-brother, a groomsman who was chatting with friends, and tossed out a little small talk. "Nice wedding."

Craig got it on video.

Chauncey knew this was his one and only Blood Brother. He asked, "Hey, can I get a picture with you?"

The guy gave Chauncey a slightly puzzled expression. But he obliged.

Chauncey explained that they were putting some pictures together for the reception.

Still, no resemblances were jumping out.

By now, almost all the guests had dispersed. With only a few total strangers standing around, Chauncey didn't want to have that deer-in-the-headlights look. They had to get to the reception, where it was easier to get lost in the crowd.

Once they arrived at the reception, they realized every table place had a name. They needed a plan, just in case. So the two befriended the DJ there, found out his name, and then discovered the name of his company. They also found out he didn't know anyone in the wedding party. Perfect.

Craig and Chauncey were now part of the DJ package. Yeah, they could help in some way.

As Chauncey mingled, he tried to ask casual questions about the father of the bride. What school did he attend? Where does he work? And he quietly logged in all the information he could.

Now the wedding party stood outside, lined up to make their entrance and be formally introduced. The bride, however, waited in her limo.

Chauncey looked at Craig. "Here goes. Make sure you don't mess up. Camera on. Lens cap off. If you've ever pushed a wrong button…"

He took a deep breath and walked up to his bio dad. Sticking out a hand, he said, "It was a beautiful wedding."

Ray shook it. "Thank you." Chauncey didn't say the words in his mind: "You have no idea you're shaking your son's hand."

Two down, one to go.

They knew getting to the bride wouldn't be easy, but they just had to give it a try.

She got out of the limo, moving in her big white gown. And she did a double take toward Chauncey and Craig. There it was, that look that said, "Who are these two?" If the bride didn't know the guests, who did?

She walked over to her mother and father and whispered something. All six eyes turned toward the unidentified guests.

Chauncey knew they were nailed and whispered fiercely, "Craig, we have to get out of here, right now." They turned, trying not to rush, and walked toward their car. No looking back. Was anyone chasing them? Whatever happened, Chauncey was determined not give up the cameras. He'd put up a big fight over that.

Chauncey felt enormous relief after the car doors locked and they drove away, full of pictures.

Back at their hotel, it began to go through Chauncey like an electric charge. This was one of the greatest things he'd ever pulled off! Job well done. Yes, he'd have this stuff forever. It was a kind of closure. (And yeah, take that, mother of the bride.)

Letting It Go

A year after crashing the wedding, one of Chauncey's Marrison half-sisters asked him, "Have you ever thought of contacting any of your Campbell siblings yourself?"

Chauncey's first response was, "No, I have to respect their wishes."

But Rita replied, "Well, if they knew they had a brother, I sure bet they'd want to know about him."

And Chauncey began to think about the rights of children, apart from their parents. These were adult kids, after all. They weren't even teenagers. Didn't they have a right to know? And didn't Chauncey have a right to know them too?

So, he made a decision. Even if it was going to upset their shared dad (because of Betty), he was going to call those siblings and let them know he existed.

Bina tracked down a sister and asked if Chauncey could call her. She sounded very accepting.

So, they talked, and she was friendly. "This is not your fault," she said. "This is about stuff our parents did a long time ago."

There was nothing to dislike about this woman. It was good to know her.

And she said she was going bowling with her mom the following night and would mention that Chauncey had called. She promised she would get back to him.

A month passed with no contact.

Chauncey called again. She still sounded friendly, but hadn't told her brother or sister about him. She said that she would, however, and that the news should come from her, as the oldest. Chauncey thought she was taking this cautious approach out of respect for her parents.

So, as more months passed without contact, Chauncey decided to let this go. He couldn't demand what wasn't going to be given.

Loss and Closure

Another two years passed, and Chauncey began to feel it important that his father know he'd been there at the wedding. So, he had Bina call him one more time.

Somehow she got him on the phone. "Remember me?"

"Yes, Bina. Unfortunately, things haven't changed. My wife just can't handle it." He asked how Chauncey was doing.

Bina told him and then dropped the news. "Chauncey wanted you to know that you met him. He and a friend went to Karen's wedding."

There was that easy chuckle again. "No way. One of the two guys there with the cameras?"

Bina heard Betty in the background, starting to lay it on her husband. He had to get off the phone.

But after Bina told Chauncey about the conversation, and after he'd pried to get every detail, every inflection, every tone of voice, out of her, he came to a pleasant conclusion. Yeah, his father was proud of him. That kid had some gumption. He must have been impressed, in his heart of hearts. That's what Chauncey read into the encounter. That's what he'd take with him.

Even though he may have been proud of Chauncey, it wasn't enough for Ray to make contact. At least he knew he'd shaken hands with his son.

Ray Campbell died of lung cancer in 2009 at the age of 66.

And for Chauncey, it was accompanied by another stroke of providence. Loretta's husband, a man Chauncey had begun to call Pop, just happened to see the obituaries one day from the town where he grew up. And there it was, the death of Ray Campbell. So, he forwarded the news to Chauncey.

Yes, it was heartbreaking at first. This was the first parent Chauncey had ever lost. And he would never have contact with him. He'd lost someone he never knew and yet loved.

But God seemed to have His hand in the news coming through.

So, Chauncey called his half-sister Lisa. "This is Chauncey. Remember me?"

Lisa gave him her father's light, good-humored chuckle.

"Look, this may be awkward, but I just wanted to say how sorry I am to hear about your dad passing." Chauncey wanted to say "our dad," but he held back.

Lisa explained about the lung cancer. Ray hadn't smoked in ages. He quit when he was thirty-five. (Chauncey remembered that he'd quit smoking at the age of thirty-five.) But he worked in a factory where a lot of people came down with lung cancer.

Lisa sounded sweet. She said she had told her brother and sister about him. She gave them his name and number.

They never called. Chauncey sent sympathy cards to all these family members but didn't hear back. There was a part of Chauncey that wanted Betty to feel guilty about getting condolences from the son she prevented her husband from seeing.

There are still a lot of questions. Missing family pieces can mean a lot to a person. They linger. Chauncey tells himself that maybe the brother and sisters will contact him after their mother passes.

The search for a biological parent can be very rewarding. In fact, there's a certain satisfaction an adopted person feels in finding that face, or those faces, even when they're not welcoming. It's closure.

There's a little bit of healing even in the face that only glances your way for a few seconds.

But it's also a myth to think that everything is automatically good news. People have histories, people have issues, people have complications. And they bring all this to bear on their encounter with a child once given up. What adopted people need to remember, and what is very hard to remember, is that the bio parent's reaction often has very, very little to do with them. It's about the parent; it's about their problems. Sometimes they just can't get past them.

But when Chauncey reflects on his journey toward Bio Dad, which ended with an anonymous encounter, something becomes clear. Even if he never found the happy ending with Loretta, even if this dad were the only story, the effort would still be worth it. He'd still be glad he'd set out on that journey toward the unknown. Even less than happy endings bring closure. And that's so important for the adopted. There's a little bit of healing even in the face that only glances your way for a few seconds.

Something to Know: My Rights, Your Rights

Throughout the history of adoption, there's always been one difficult question to resolve: What's more important, the right of an adopted child to know who his or her biological parents are or the right of parents who gave up a child to remain anonymous?

Legally, things have been tipping toward the adopted child for a while. But still, there can be plenty of roadblocks. For example, Betty's issues trumped everything else when a kid from some past relationship threatened to come into her husband's life. Some people can't imagine shutting out a human being like that. Other people can't imagine welcoming some "mistake" into their present.

But what about the rights of siblings, especially when they're grown? Does the adopted individual have a right to seek them out, to make contact? Wouldn't they want to know about this blood brother or sister?

And one of the reasons people don't recognize the rights of the adopted is a persistent myth. Something that says, "You're over it."

A lot of people think that a child can be told he or she is adopted at an early age but also told he or she was chosen and loved and will always be cared for, and that's it. You break the news in a good way, and you move on.

It's true that adopted kids in a loving home will move on; they'll be able to lead normal lives. But it's a myth that the issue is resolved, period. You can be a smiling, happy individual, but in the background, there's that good-bye and those unknown birth parents. It's there. And it will make some waves in your life.

You're never completely over it. And the more you suppress all acknowledgement that it's there, the more it will haunt you.

Chauncey, for example, would look back on his own control issues and see a connection to who he was as an adopted individual.

Sometimes it happened with Bina, when he'd talk trash about some good-looking guy she had taken an interest in. She wondered why he was so upset.

Looking back, she'd realize it wasn't because Chauncey wanted to be the boyfriend. It was because he had to be number one in the relationship. Was she now going to spend all her time with this new beau and leave him out of the picture?

That question popped up in Chauncey's head in various ways with friends over the years. He had a gift for friendship. No denying that. He cared about people. But in time, his buddies would get girlfriends or wives, his gal pals would get boyfriends or husbands. And Chauncey's time with them would decrease dramatically.

Well, Chauncey wasn't so good at finding that significant other. He'd filled his life with significant others. And he couldn't stand the idea of being cut off. More accurately, he had a hard time settling for being number two. Chauncey was quite persistent in his quest: "You've got to make time for me too!" He often managed to get his closest friends to set aside one night during the week to hang out with him—even after they were married.

And yes, there was flack from spouses on occasion. Chauncey tried not to think about the fights he might be causing. Once in a while, his special friends might even say, "You're worse than my husband!" or, "You're more demanding than my wife!"

And much later, Chauncey would realize that what drove him was that haunting question, "Will I ever be number one in a big relationship?" There's something about a lot of adopted people that prevents them from feeling like they're number one, even when they're loved and cherished by parents. And in that insecure terrain, it's fairly easy to fall into the trap of trying to control other people so they'll let you play an irreplaceable role in their lives.

You don't let go of others because there's something inside that just won't let go of you. It's the frailty inside that makes you grab so tightly on to something outside. It's the mushiness in your own identity that can make you have to put in concrete your expectations of others.

You do have to choose your level of exposure.

Because of his soap-star friends, and his work in marketing TV shows, Chauncey had plenty of connections. So, when people in Hollywood started hearing about his reunion with Loretta, a few different TV shows asked him to appear as a guest.

You don't let go of others because there's something inside that just won't let go of you.

Chauncey was still swimming through the intense emotions of that whole experience. There were still days when it just seemed too much, and he had to retreat to his condo for a while and just nap or play video games. His reaction was, "If I think I'm stressed out now, imagine what it would be like sharing the story on a national talk show!"

The prospect seemed way too overwhelming. So, Chauncey declined, despite his exciting experiences on the edge of the soap-star spotlight.

Besides, he thought he looked kind of ugly when bawling. Why put that on the screen?

Everybody has their own take on getting the story into broad daylight. Everybody's history attaches to that door into a new chapter of life. So, everybody has to make their own choices.

Chapter 9

Two Moms

Chauncey was trying to prepare for the moment when his two mothers would meet. There was a lot to think about. There was more to feel than he could get his heart around.

He always thought about what Mom Marilyn would think and feel more than anybody else. Her heart was biggest in his mind. Yet he was also aware that his journey had affected a wide circle of people.

Up until the age of thirty-six, Chauncey had assumed he'd live the rest of his life with one mom, one dad, one brother, one sister. But now he'd discovered seven sisters, two brothers, two moms, two dads, a stepmom, and a stepdad. And there seemed to be countless new aunts, uncles, cousins, nieces, and nephews. Each one of them, to a greater or lesser extent, was dealing with this adoption event. It reverberated.

Mother's Day was more complicated now. True, Marilyn's card wasn't a challenge. All the ones that talked about how much Mom had meant to him through the years fit quite well. But how do you find a Mother's Day card for the woman you just met? Chauncey would stand in a store and look at one card after another, with all those sweet lines: "you were always there for me"; "all my life"; "who I am today."

Nothing fit. It took quite a search to find something that would honor Loretta, instead of reminding her of what she'd missed. Chauncey made a note to himself: "patent bio mom card and send to Hallmark."

Two Mothers, One Son

Chauncey's two moms did have one conversation already on the phone. It was that first mutual Mother's Day, and Chauncey wanted to introduce them.

Loretta told Marilyn, "Thank you for taking care of my boy."

Marilyn said, "Thanking for making it possible, letting us have him."

Short conversations. So much in the hearts behind them.

When Loretta walked into the Smith home in Newbury Park, California, she was clutching Rita's arm. And this daughter could feel how nervous her mother was on the big occasion. But when they were all introduced, she didn't show it.

Two mothers hugging—a simple thing. Not much bawling. But so much life had gone through those two hearts pressed together. Too much to think about, really. And yet through all their interaction Rita never caught the slightest hint of competition or discomfort about whose son this actually was.

As they talked and snacked and met one friend after another, what stood out was how happy every single person was that Chauncey had decided to contact his bio mom.

Chauncey wanted this to be a party in honor of Bina. She was the one, after all, who put in all the hours to make this possible. So, he made sure everyone was introduced to her and everyone knew the role she played.

And he also found himself still doing it, still staring, still taking in similarities. His sisters, his bio mom. The way Leigh Ann moved around the kitchen, the curve of Rita's fingers on someone's

> ### Marilyn: "If I Were Adopted, I'd Want to Find That Too"
>
> The most rewarding thing for me was seeing that Chauncey had this whole extended family who really loved him. For thirty-five years, a kid can't help but wonder about all that. And now there were all these people excited to have found him. Mother, sisters, uncles, and aunts. If I were adopted, I'd want to find that too.

shoulder, the expression Loretta had when greeting people—how many times she blinked per minute, for pity's sake. It was a continuing secret spectacle.

> ## It was the caress of flesh and blood that had been absent for so many years.

And the funny thing was that every bit of recognition, every little sign of "there's my DNA," felt like healing. It was the caress of flesh and blood that had been absent for so many years.

A couple of nights later, Chauncey had an event that rivaled the great Ohio welcome the Marrison clan had put on. Some of Chauncey's many, many friends gathered at Chuck and Marilyn's home to meet the new family. Now Loretta was really getting a feel for California. Some of them had even been soap stars.

There was Bina, who had invested so much time in tracking Loretta down, starting with just a name on a birth certificate. There was Chauncey's family and friends.

Rita realized there was a lot more catching up to do than she'd imagined.

Bina had been struck by Rita as well; she seemed to resemble Chauncey the most. Her lifelong friend was indeed Loretta's flesh and blood. She basked in the fruit of her labors. You couldn't have asked for a better outcome.

And what Bina picked up on was that Chauncey didn't just have gestures and behaviors that reflected this or that about the Marrisons. He seemed to be picking them up as he went along, noticing more and more things, and, yes, reflecting them back. He was expressing those traits they had in common with more and more confidence. It was like Chauncey was expanding himself before her eyes.

Family and Faith

As Chauncey looked at his two moms interacting and at all the other friends and relatives in the room getting to know each other, he couldn't help reflecting on the values he'd absorbed. All these conversations in his parents' house, flowing back and forth, all this interaction. All these family traits floating around.

But there was something more than facial features or gestures to recognize here. There were also the basic values that had made him the man he was. And they flowed from Chuck and Marilyn, Mom and Dad, happy hosts at the moment in their home.

"Yeah," Chauncey realized with a sigh, "I was raised well. I was taught well. I watched Mom and Dad live by the golden rule." Sure, he dreaded having to go to church with them as a teen. Sure, he wasn't excited about attending church school. Growing up in a conservative Christian environment, he could tell his family was different from the families of most of his friends.

But it had all left him with one very important Friend. Wasn't there a line in a hymn: "My constant friend is He"? Yes, somehow God had developed for Chauncey into that reliable companion, someone on whom you could count.

Chauncey wasn't clear precisely how it happened. But He was there. And it was one of the gifts he could cherish the most at this point. Thanks, Mom and Dad.

He hadn't been the greatest churchgoer in the world, not exactly obedient to the denomination's ever rule and regulation. There seemed to be an infinite number of them when he was a kid. Pretty scary stuff. (Now at least he knew there were only ten!)

But what do you know, here he was at the age of thirty-six, and his faith was alive and well. He sensed it most keenly in music. Some Christian songs, in fact, blew him away. There were lines that reverberated inside like some ancient creed that believers recited for centuries.

A lot of thoughts jostled around in his head as Chauncey looked on this family scene, a family cobbled together in midlife. A lot of emotions pushed here and there inside him. And yes, sometimes it was a little much; he had to go into the bathroom and take a deep breath.

But over all that was this simple, basic reality: faith didn't seem hard at all. And for the first time in his life, Chauncey realized he was proud to be a Christian.

Something to Know: Values Win Out

Fitting in is always going to be huge for an adopted person. They can't escape that. It's in their bones. And they always wonder where they got this trait from, where they got that tendency from. It's much more of a mystery to solve for the adopted.

As you sort through a new family, finding some uncle with your red hair or a grandparent with your quirky ears can be great fun.

But through all this, many adopted individuals begin to see one thing stand out: it's the values they absorbed that shaped them. The values are what makes them who they are.

And people who care for adopted kids can take comfort in that. We can't always give people on a journey toward their bio mom a happy ending. They won't always feel they fit in with a family, even if it is their own flesh and blood. Sometimes they get stuck with a dead end.

But what we can give kids whose identity is a bit more precarious are essential building blocks: the building blocks of character. We can help them see what matters are the qualities that make relationships rewarding.

We can show them that love needs to be at the center of everything.

We can teach them that boundaries can give them a stronger sense of self, not just a way to conform.

We can teach them that courtesy and kindness in the face of an often-calloused world can make you stronger, not weaker.

We can teach them that selfishness is the real dead end and that a consistent concern for others opens up so much of the goodness of life.

We can teach them that it's

But what we can give kids whose identity is a bit more precarious are essential building blocks: the building blocks of character.

really a heavenly Father who stands at the beginning and the end of their journey of discovery. And that can make all the difference.

Strong values are what a person can hang on to as they go down a bumpy road toward their past. People need to have a core concept of who they are if they are going to stretch in a positive way.

Chauncey would always remember the values Sandi Patty expressed when he introduced her to Loretta at a concert in North Carolina. In the midst of a big, teary embrace she whispered, "Thank you for choosing life."

He would feel values when Marilyn shared lyrics with him from a Sandi Patty song she loved. She knew her son would one day walk with his biological family. And she cherished her time of nurture with him all the more for that reason.

One thing that stands out in Marilyn's mind as she reflects on the journey her son has taken is that he has remained such a loyal and caring son. She expresses it rather modestly: "if your kids grow up and like you a bit, it's wonderful. If they like you a lot, it's even better." What she doesn't say is that the very loyalty and caring that she finds so rewarding as a parent are qualities that reflect her character and Chuck's character. They are strong values that sunk in over the years to the boy they always called their own— and were willing to let go.

Chapter 10

Greg

Greg just didn't want to know the answer. He didn't want to try to find out.

When Chauncey told his buddy about finding Loretta, Greg wept for days and was full of questions. He was happy for the happy ending. But that somehow made him even more afraid that his story might turn out badly. He was convinced closure couldn't happen for him.

Greg had been adopted by loving, Christian parents, just like Chauncey. He'd grown up in a stable home. After the two met at a work-related party, they resonated with each other's stories. Chauncey understood when Greg talked about how he'd argued with his sister as a kid: "You always get the bigger piece of pie because you're their real child."

"No, you get the biggest scoop of ice cream because you're adopted."

Chauncey had those kinds of feelings about his brother, Barry, the "real child" of the family. Adopted kids are keenly aware of anything that might signal they're on the outside. Birth kids start to think the adopted one gets a lot more special attention.

Chauncey and Greg were both thirty-five and both loved the Lakers and jet skis. They attended concerts, everything from the Heritage Singers to KISS, and had something big in common: partying. Greg was even more outgoing that his friend and typically became the life of whatever party he attended. He had the social shtick that could rival Chauncey's hanging-with-soap-stars days.

But Greg seemed to take things to the edge. Chauncey began to look like the stable one by comparison. Greg hated being alone. He went through women at a rather frightening speed. And he drank with what seemed like a vengeance.

Over time, Chauncey found himself frequently trying to help his friend, the alcoholic. His binges wiped him out.

The two got to know each other well during the time Greg grieved over his mother's death. All kinds of feelings surfaced after the funeral. Greg felt like the black sheep of the family. He'd never lived up to his parents' expectations. Parents like that deserved a much better son. They were in church; he was out chasing girls.

Chauncey tried to encourage him. There was a lot more to Greg than just his drinking and partying. Once, during a social event at one of the Christian telecasts Chauncey worked for, Greg had rescued him. It was a time when Chauncey hadn't yet kicked his secret smoking habit. And he cheerfully walked into the gathering, oblivious to the pack of cigarettes in his shirt pocket. Greg quietly and deftly snatched the pack away and held it in his hand. He didn't work for the church, so it wouldn't matter if they saw him with the smokes.

But something kept Greg down. Something kept him going back to the bottle, even though he seemed to have a happy, successful life. Greg got a great job in Maryland working as a manager at a floral arrangement distributor, a company that provided stores with artificial plants and flowers. He was in charge of all the contracts with big chain stores around the country. And he'd finally settled down and married a sweet, lovely woman named Amy. Why did he have this need to slam himself out of consciousness?

At one point, Chauncey brought Greg to Nashville for a Christian concert Chauncey was promoting. They were put up in a nice hotel, but through the night, Chauncey kept waking up to the sound of beer cans opening. And there Greg sat, on the other bed in the dark, swigging a can. Chauncey didn't take it well. He had to be bright and alert for the interaction with concert people the next day; he hated being kept awake.

So, Chauncey yelled. He even used the word "alcoholic" for the first time.

Greg yelled back. He wasn't. He could stop anytime.

There was also an edge to Chauncey's anger he wouldn't recognize until sometime later. He had been given up for adoption basically because of someone's alcoholism and abusive behavior. The man Loretta was with when she became pregnant had ruled himself out as a potential father for that reason. Loretta simply couldn't bring a child into a world where a man constantly leaned on the bottle and regularly dumped his anger on her.

And Chauncey had to watch as his friend sunk into that stage of nonlife. Before, Greg could sell his drinking as just a part of his oversized social life. And he was a lot of fun at parties. But now, Chauncey realized, weekend binges had become Monday-through-Friday streams of liquor. Greg was even hiding bottles at work. His coworkers began to detect more and more lies scattered around to hide his habit.

When Bina was playing Sherlock Holmes for Chauncey, engaged in the long process of tracking down Loretta, the two kept Greg up-to-date. He was always hopeful about the outcome. But when Bina offered to help Greg find his bio mom, he always waved his hand. Chauncey encouraged him to do it too. But Greg was not going there.

Two nurturing human beings had raised this man. What gave him such a fear of rejection? What made him determined not to set out on a journey with a question mark at the end?

It was one of those things that baffled Chauncey. He had come to know his buddy well. They had a lot of good times together. And yes, that instinctive fear of abandonment, that insecurity about family in general, and his status as a son in particular—all those things Chauncey understood completely. But still, he couldn't get anywhere near a clear reason for that shut door.

The bottle even knocked over Greg's marriage. He kept wanting to go out clubbing with Chauncey instead of spending time at home with his wife. She never understood that.

Chauncey did see qualities of loyalty and friendship in Greg that few others noticed. Adopted people who share stories have a bond that even wives and girlfriends can't understand. They both knew they'd never have kids. But he also felt guilty about what was happening with Greg's marriage. Still, for a long time, it just seemed like guys having good times.

But eventually, Greg drank himself out of affection, out of attention, out of time, out of meaningful interaction. In time, the two-guys-partying relationship changed. Chauncey found himself taking care of Greg more and more, picking him up from some drunken stupor, lending him money, listening to lists of woes.

They'd talked about everything. There were moments when Greg could confess his compulsion to promiscuity. Why would he sit down at a restaurant with friends and show off close-ups of his girlfriend's body parts to people? What was that about?

And Chauncey could confess his own times of sexual ambiguity. Nothing seemed that clear-cut for the adopted. They have a higher rate of nonstandard sexuality.

But now Greg was turning into a miserable, highly unstable human being. Alcohol even provoked a mean streak in him at times. Chauncey would tell Greg that he never acted nice to Amy. She seemed a saint by comparison, even though she carried around this withering anger about the way her husband treated her.

Amy pleaded and threatened for a long time. Eventually, however, she moved from Maryland back to California. And in the aftermath, Greg's craziness turned to disaster. He was to stand up as best man at a wedding. Another of his "best friends" was getting married. But the night before the ceremony, Greg slept with the bride.

Chauncey blew up when he heard about it. "How could you do that to your friend?"

Greg excused it at just a one-night thing; the couple was having problems anyway.

Eventually, the ambivalent bride would divorce her husband and move in with Greg. That relationship lasted a couple of rough years. Greg knew he was a bad husband and would make a terrible father. But he hated being alone; there had to be someone else in the house for him.

"We'll Talk Tomorrow"

Chauncey felt compelled to go to the store and get some groceries for his friend. Greg had nothing in his rented room but a bottle of vodka. Chauncey stocked his kitchen with a week's supply of food—and wondered if he was being an enabler.

He sat with Greg a while, told him he loved him as a friend. It was very hard to watch the pain and gloom steal across his face—and his whole body. But Greg still wouldn't seek the real help he desperately needed. Greg had been mentioning for a few weeks that he was going to kill himself. He would even call Chauncey at night and say good-bye. Chauncey begged Greg to get help; he even agreed to go with him to a counselor or hospital.

Chauncey felt very, very tired. Was it depression? He'd seen an electric cord hanging from a rod in the closet. That's where Greg had supposedly been trying to hang himself. Chauncey stared at it. The current Greg wasn't the man he'd known all these years, the life of the party, the good friend.

And Chauncey just couldn't drag Greg out of this self-destructive cave. Why was he determined to stay there?

Chauncey left, saying, "We'll talk tomorrow."

Collateral Damage

A few nights later, Chauncey got an out-of-town call from Greg's family, asking if he could retrieve his valuables. The landlord, fed up with the perpetually delayed rent, had had him evicted and was threatening to throw Greg's possessions away. And Greg wasn't around. His antics had caught the attention of authorities. He was staying in a detox facility in downtown LA, confined because police had concluded he was a threat to himself and others.

So, in the middle of this night, Chauncey drug himself over to the house with a friend and loaded everything up. Walking all those boxes to his car, Chauncey couldn't stop thinking about how Greg had been talking suicide the last couple of weeks. He kept referring to that electric cord dangling in the closet.

And Chauncey recalled all the times he'd begged Greg to get help. He just had to check himself into a serious rehab facility. Only Greg himself could do that.

It was very painful to think about one of Greg's last requests. He wanted his buddy to come over and stay with him. But Chauncey had concluded he just couldn't play the enabler and the rescuer anymore. He tried hard to get his friend to face the hard reality. Suicide had collateral damage. *Who's going to find your body?*

So, as he put the last of the boxes in his trunk, Chauncey felt the anger seething. His back hurt. How many times had he done this?

At five the next morning, Greg apparently was released from detox and walked home. The landlady saw him on her way to work and called the owner of the home. "Be prepared for trouble."

Greg probably walked by the trash cans where some of his expendable possessions had been thrown. He tried to get in the door to his room, but the locks had been changed. He must have looked in the window and seen the empty room. He had absolutely nothing left. The landlord had forgotten to put a note on his door saying Chauncey had his stuff. This would haunt Chauncey terribly in the weeks ahead. If only Greg had read a note. Would that have made a difference? His possessions hadn't been thrown away.

Greg hung himself over a fence, five feet from the front door.

Saying Good-Bye Again

Chauncey got a call at work at 11:00 a.m. Someone had found Greg and tried unsuccessfully to revive him.

Chauncey's first reaction was simple numbness. So much pain and anguish and sadness had already passed between them. What was he supposed to feel now?

He had to call two of Greg's closest friends and tell them. He had to call Amy.

Chauncey worked the rest of the day at his office, without telling his coworkers anything. He couldn't. He had to stay busy. He couldn't let it sink in.

But when Chauncey got home to his condo, there it was, all of Greg's stuff he'd brought over the night before. Everything was laid out in the living room, including the CDs he wanted Chauncey to have.

The disaster began to bowl him over. His only consolation was that the last good-bye was a good one. At least he hadn't chewed Greg out about his life.

That loss of life didn't really hit Chauncey until the funeral service a week later. Not until he pulled up in the parking lot and saw Amy walking to the gravesite. Chauncey drove slowly past the people gathering there and began sobbing, harder and harder, until he felt he was becoming ill.

Chauncey knew Greg had been reading his Bible right up to the time he committed suicide. So, Chauncey focused on God knowing the heart, on grace, on some kind of hope. Greg had drunk his wife away; he'd even drunk all his girlfriends away. He'd drunk until he had absolutely nothing left except the bottle. He just couldn't take the pain and stress of being alone.

Chauncey grabbed hold of a song at the funeral for all he was worth. It was a beautiful tune, and the lyrics described running through fields of laughter. Chauncey felt the power of God in that hymn; he felt an assurance that this heavenly Father would get him through the hard grief, the loss, the inexplicable disaster of Greg's end.

Maybe he would find peace now. Maybe somehow now he could find a healing that had eluded him every day of his life.

Something to Know: You Still Have Choices

Adopted people can have dramatically different outcomes.
The bio mom or bio dad can bring you closure, resolution.
They can remain a mystery.
They can turn out to be pretty scary characters.

That's the drama of looking for your people of origin—or avoiding them.

But through all that journey, one thing remains crucially true. Our individual choices still matter. They matter a great deal. We may have to struggle with all kinds of tricky feelings. We may have to deal with pressures and longings that other people can only vaguely understand.

But adopted people still have choices, just like everybody else. And sometimes their choices can send them on vastly different highways.

Yes, everybody has to own their life circumstances. A person can exploit the fact that they're adopted as well as be shaped by it.

Greg's life didn't end tragically just because he didn't set out on that journey toward his birth parents. It didn't end that way just because his mystery of origin endured.

It ended because Greg's choices couldn't push up against the darker forces inside, forces that were destroying him. He couldn't or didn't take steps in the opposite direction from that tide that was taking him out to a dark sea. He didn't, in the end, wave his hand for help.

Everybody can get stuck in ruts. And everybody's rut gets deeper over time. That's why we're given choices at crucial times in our lives. Are we just going to go with the flow, or will we make an effort to get to a better place?

Are we just going to go with the flow, or will we make an effort to get to a better place?

Chauncey would anguish for months after Greg's death about the circumstances. There would be a lot of "Why Greg? Why not me?" He didn't feel that he somehow deserved this happy ending with Loretta. He didn't think it had come to him because he was a couple of steps above Greg.

What he saw most was how much Greg and he had in common, how much their lives had intersected. And yet the outcomes? So dramatically different?

Life does remain largely a mystery. We probably won't know the answers to a lot of big questions until we get up there and run through those fields of laughter and ask the heavenly Father about our perplexities. Yet through these two lives, one theme does run and stand out: choices. They may not have seemed huge at the time. They may not even have seemed that dramatically different. But yes, over the long term, they did lead down opposite paths.

BIO Family

Smith Family

Chapter 11

Steven

"Why not make it simple? Just ask for directions. You're lost in Victorville. You're confused. Get her to come outside and point down the street here and there, and you can get your pictures."

Driving on the way to Las Vegas, Steven and Chauncey had been talking about ways to get the other bio mom on camera. It was his sister Char's mom, the woman who did not want contact. But Chauncey knew how meaningful it was to have another face in this world you could look at and recognize your own features. So, he just had to try to get a photo somehow.

But how to do it? She probably wouldn't be that friendly. They tossed out several ideas, from taking a survey to asking about houses for sale in the area. But Steven's suggestion of directions seemed to work.

Bina was in another car with a friend. Steven drove down the street a block and parked. They'd decided Bina should walk up to the door and ask how to get to the 15 Highway going north. A woman asking for directions would be less threatening. Chauncey would stand on the sidewalk, pretend to be taking pictures of the area, and hopefully get a few shots of the woman.

They rehearsed their lines.

They checked to make sure everything was OK with the camera.

Steven even said a little prayer down the street.

Bina knocked on the door.

Nobody home.

Windows into Adoption

Chauncey and Steven had become friends when both were single, both working at the media center. Steven had freelanced as a writer and producer for many years. He was going through some midlife rebellion after his divorce and after a very strict upbringing. And Chauncey seemed to understand quite well. He was a different kind of guy friend. One who was very fun to hang with and, yes, party with, and also sensitive.

And what struck Steven as he followed Chauncey on his journey toward Bio Mom was how deeply everything affected Chauncey (or more accurately, how openly he expressed the intense emotions he was going through).

Steven first encountered adoption when he was in his early twenties. A friend of his seemed obsessed with finding her biological parents. The girl had a decent mom and dad who'd raised her well. She seemed to have a good home life. So, in the back of his mind, Steven was thinking, "What's the big deal? Your parents are your parents, period. That's all you know. Who really cares who your biological ones are?"

Steven imagined he wouldn't need to find anyone else besides the mom and dad who raised him to complete his life. He was good to go. Out of the oven, so to speak. Raised with love and nurture.

But later, it struck him. "The reason I can't imagine wanting to find my 'real' parents is precisely because I have them already," Steven thought. "Growing up with the people who gave me birth has given me a kind of security that makes it easy for me to feel independent, settled, whole. There are no missing pieces. And that's precisely why I don't instinctively resonate with folks who have an undying hankering to connect with biology."

As it turns out, biology not only helps us feel secure in various ways. It also keeps us from fully entering into the experience of those without it.

But sometimes we do get windows. Sometimes we do get a glimpse, something that makes us catch our breath

And that's when Steven got a little window into what Chauncey must have been going through. He revisited the scene Chauncey had described so vividly in Loretta's home. He remembered the feelings his buddy had experienced going through one rendezvous after another.

It matters when someone resonates with an experience that's difficult to share, an experience not that many people have in common. And in following Chauncey through this journey toward Bio Mom, Steven realized something in the end. There *are* ways you can enter into this experience that's not your own. We're all given windows, of one kind or another, that help us see into the heart of the journey, not just the details.

There are ways you can enter into this experience that's not your own.

Something to Know: From the Outside Looking In

In documenting Chauncey's story, what Steven picked up most of all is this: there is quite a bit to admire in this journey. There's quite a bit to learn from there.

He has seen it in the way Chauncey and Loretta have dealt with very difficult emotions. Being the typical guy who's happy with a good job and an occasional game of football, he doesn't naturally *get* all those complicated emotions. And yet it's pretty impressive to see these two people work through them. Loretta had buried intense feelings about that lost child for decades so that she could give her husband and her daughters a happy, untroubled life. She hadn't suppressed her feelings for no reason.

So dragging them up, as she went over the details of the whole story, was a formidable task. She couldn't handle the feelings back then. How was she supposed to handle them now, when they'd only grown bigger underground?

Chauncey himself was tiptoeing around a minefield of emotions as *So That's Who I Am* bounced around with questions he hadn't been able to ask for decades, questions Loretta had been afraid to answer for decades. He was terrified of hurting Loretta. He just had to know about the day he was given up.

But in the end, they talked through it. They felt the loss. They looked at the pain through each other's tears. And they bonded in the present tense. It was hard. And it was wonderful.

That's a kind of courage even a typical guy can admire.

After Loretta went through her answers to difficult questions with Chauncey for her chapter, something she'd been dreading for months, her first reaction was, "Oh, is that all?"

It wasn't the wrenching, hurtful experience she had feared. It was more like a huge weight off. She said she wished she had done this a lot earlier.

But she also said she could never have done it alone. She needed Chauncey there, a very understanding, loving son, to plunge back into the moment of giving up.

Chauncey has been told by counselors that, at some point, he is going to feel real anger toward Bio Mom. It's a natural, healthy emotion people have to go through. You're going to have to express some of those feelings about the one who gave you up, get them out.

Maybe a lot of folks do. But, for whatever reason, Chauncey just didn't have to go there. He was expressing plenty of emotions, to be sure. He wasn't repressing any that he could even remotely get his hands on. But looking back on that day of his birth when he was exchanged from one mom to another, he still feels quite lucky and blessed. He was loved and cherished by the parents who raised him. And he can see clearly why Loretta, in her circumstances, thought adoption the best alternative.

Perhaps the thing Steven came to admire the most was the way Chauncey tried so hard to give the closure that he'd experienced to someone else, his sister Char.

Sometime after that knock on the door in Victorville when no one was home, Chauncey tried again, during another road trip. He drove up to the bio mom's street—by himself this time. He'd tried to get a glimpse a few other times as well with no luck. This time, Chauncey observed two other cars parked in the driveway. He stopped a few houses away and waited, holding a video camera he'd borrowed from a friend.

After several minutes, two ladies came out. He couldn't make out their faces very clearly. But he did overhear one say, "Your flowers look so pretty." OK, that meant one of them was the homeowner.

Soon, a third lady came out and started talking about going to the grocery store. Chauncey thought this was his chance.

The ladies got in a car, and Chauncey began to follow from a distance, doing his best "Columbo" imitation. When it became clear they were going to Albertson's, he pulled ahead and parked first, just in case they suspected he was following them.

Inside, Chauncey noticed that one of the ladies was in her sixties, the age Char's bio mom would be. And yes, he vaguely recognized the face that had appeared at the door five years before when he delivered that letter.

He grabbed a cart and started down the aisles behind the ladies, tossing in vegetables at random, most of which he couldn't even name. Now he knew who he had to focus on.

Chauncey had a plan. The little video camera, fortunately, didn't look that different from a cell phone. So, if the ladies ever turned around while he was shooting them, he would pretend like he was talking on the phone, asking someone whether it was potatoes or tomatoes that they'd asked for.

So, he pushed his cart up and down aisles, sometimes behind the ladies, sometimes ahead of them, getting a string of video clips, getting as close as he could without arousing any fears.

Chauncey had to put quite a bit into his cart. But he managed to stay fairly close to the ladies all the way to the cashier. When things got a bit tight, he said out loud to himself in an embarrassed voice, "Oh, my wallet!" and rushed out to the car.

As soon as Chauncey got back home, he had a friend make a DVD copy and sent it off to Char. Now, at last, she could see and hear what her mom looked like and sounded like. She would watch it countless times, trying to pick up little bits of herself. It was something concrete about her origin she could hold in her hands.

Char's thank-you resonated deeply, of course. He knew how much it meant to her. Words can't begin to describe. But he did have that Bio Dad video. And he knew what that had done for him.

These days, when Chauncey sits with Loretta on her back porch in Locust, North Carolina, looking out at squirrels in the oak trees, cardinals in the bird feeder, flowers in the garden, a picnic table in the shade, he is still in awe of his journey, still amazed at how things worked out. Seven years after the rendezvous, he is still taking a deep breath of thankfulness.

But those close to him, like Steven, are also moved by the kind of giving that can take place through this scary journey into the unknown. It's the emotional investment that Chauncey, and countless other adopted people, have made that sticks with people. People who were cut off, on some undeniable level, in the beginning, can give so much in the end. They can stretch out and touch family and find closure, even with family members who don't want to be touched.

Steven can't think of a more meaningful gift any brother has given his sister. That little jumpy video of a few ladies looking at melons and bananas at Albertson's speaks volumes about what it means to get in touch—by whatever means possible.

There's a profound need for connection in every human heart. There's an undeniable urge to get back to your roots.

There's a profound need for connection in every human heart.

There's an undeniable urge to get back to your roots. True, sometimes you can't get back all the way. Sometimes you can't get a clear picture of a face. But it's the spirit of the journey that counts the most. It's that reaching out that stretches you the farthest. And almost everyone can find closure in some way. A very big part of Chauncey's happy ending is simply his desire to share with others something that he's received.

Sometimes, the most powerful connections in life are the ones we give away.

Barry, Linda, Chuck, Marilyn, Charmaine and Chauncey.

Epilogue

Good-bye Mom

My mom Marilyn passed away on Nov. 4th 2015. This was by far the hardest, saddest thing I have ever gone through. So strange, having to end the book this way. She knew the book was done, but not published yet.

It's an understatement to say I loved her. We were very close. We were great friends and talked or saw each other almost every day. I will cherish that. Now, besides my own loss, watching Dad miss the love of his life is heartbreaking. They were married over 50 years. I take comfort in knowing that she wasn't afraid to die. Her faith was solid and Dad, Char, Barry, and I were with her, holding hands and praying when she took her last breath.

NO more fear and NO more PAIN. She is resting, waiting for Jesus to come again.

Mom welcomed everyone in my bio family. She called my bio sisters her daughters from North Carolina and they called her their California mom.

So, I'm back to buying only one Mother's Day card again. I have to admit it's strange..hard..sad -yet I'm feeling blessed. She would always say to me, "Did you remember to send Loretta a Mother's Day card?" "Did you call her?" Yes, Mom, I remembered and will continue to remember.

Chauncey

TEACH Services, Inc.
P U B L I S H I N G

We invite you to view the complete
selection of titles we publish at:
www.TEACHServices.com

We encourage you to write us
with your thoughts about this,
or any other book we publish at:
info@TEACHServices.com

TEACH Services' titles may be purchased in
bulk quantities for educational, fund-raising,
business, or promotional use.
bulksales@TEACHServices.com

Finally, if you are interested in seeing
your own book in print, please contact us at:
publishing@TEACHServices.com
We are happy to review your manuscript at no charge.

CPSIA information can be obtained
at www.ICGtesting.com
Printed in the USA
BVHW020142180222
629238BV00006B/240